SOMETHING NEW!

THE ETHNIC ENTERTAINING COOKBOOK

Minnetonka, Minnesota

SOMETHING NEW!
THE ETHNIC ENTERTAINING COOKBOOK

Printed in 2010.

Tom Carpenter
Creative Director

Jennifer Weaverling
Managing Editor

Wendy Holdman
Cover Design

Julie Cisler
Senior Book Design and Production

Phil Aarrestad
Commissioned Photography

Robin Krause
Prop Stylist, Food Stylist

Abby Wyckoff
Food Stylist

Susan Telleen
Assistant Food Stylist

On the Cover:
Flavors of Mexico menu, pp. 34–41

On the Back:
Rolled Sushi with Smoked Salmon
    and Avocado, pp. 108–109
Chorizo and Egg Empanadas with
    Avocado Salsa, pp. 138–139
Indonesian Beef Satay with Peanut
    Sauce, pp. 110–111

1 2 3 4 5 6 7 8 9 10 11 12 13 / 13 12 11 10
© 2010 Cooking Club of America
ISBN 978-1-58159-484-3

COOKING CLUB OF AMERICA
12301 Whitewater Drive
Minnetonka, MN 55343
www.cookingclub.com

CONTENTS

It's Time For

SOMETHING NEW!
THE ETHNIC ENTERTAINING COOKBOOK

For anyone passionate about the cooking arts, entertaining can be a true adventure. And whether it's a family celebration, a casual get-together with friends or a formal dinner party you want to pull off with style and taste ... the food you create is going to be the event's centerpiece.

ITALY

Roasted Asparagus with Parmigiano and Garlic Bread Crumbs, page 174

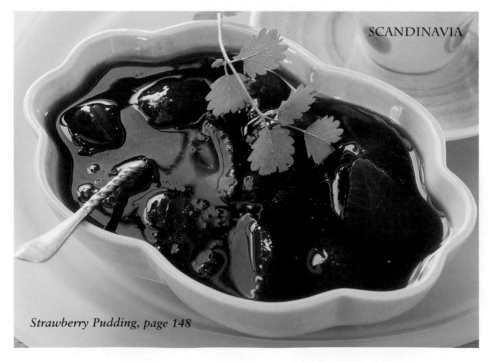

SCANDINAVIA

Strawberry Pudding, page 148

So then you start thinking — what should I cook? My old standbys? Or something new! Of course, the adventure lies in something new; so does the reward.

What better place to go than a proven and taste-filled ethnic tradition to find the new ideas you need? You'll expand your cooking horizons and delight your guests.

That's why we created *Something New! The Ethnic Entertaining Cookbook*, exclusively for Cooking Club of America Members. Here are 20 incredible and diverse menus (over a hundred recipes in all) from a variety of wonderful ethnic traditions. You will travel the culinary globe — from Italy, France, Asia and Mexico (of course!) to less-touted but equally interesting fare from Greece, India,

FRANCE

Roulade à L'orange, pages 72-73

Morocco, Spain, Scandinavia, Germany and Great Britain. In some of the countries, you'll even go to regions within — Provence in France and Mexico's Yucatan to name a couple — for great culinary ideas and insights.

It's all about *Something New* — food, fun and laughter from exciting ethnic traditions around the world. Enjoy the journey, savor the adventure!

GERMANY

Hasenpfeffer, page 95

Cooking Club
of
America ®

SIT-DOWN ASIAN DINNER

Jean Yueh

CRISPY FRIED SHRIMP BALLS WITH SWEET AND TANGY SAUCE | STIR-FRIED CHICKEN WITH PEANUTS

This menu is planned so that the host or hostess can do all the preparation and part of the cooking ahead of time.

Cook shrimp balls ahead and reheat in the oven. Cook the eggplants ahead and serve at room temperature. Make the fruit ahead and keep chilled in the refrigerator.

You can prepare the rice and chicken dishes up to half a day ahead. Just before serving, quickly stir-fry the rice and cook the chicken dish. Then sit down with your guests to enjoy the evening!

GRILLED EGGPLANTS WITH BASIL | HOME STYLE FRIED RICE | MELONS IN MINT AND GINGER INFUSION

CRISPY FRIED SHRIMP BALLS* WITH SWEET AND TANGY SAUCE

Coating the uncooked shrimp balls with coarse bread crumbs makes a delicious variation from the plain ones. These are crunchy outside and tender inside. Look for ready-made Japanese bread crumbs, labeled "Panko crumbs," at an Asian market. Or use white bread and make your own crumbs at least 2 days ahead.

FILLING

1 lb. shelled, deveined uncooked medium shrimp, halved
2 teaspoons minced fresh ginger
2 large green onions (white parts only), cut into 2-inch sections
8 large water chestnuts
2 teaspoons cornstarch
1³/4 teaspoons salt or to taste
1¼ teaspoons sugar
1 tablespoon dry sherry
1 tablespoon Asian sesame oil or vegetable oil
1 egg white

COATING

1½ cups Panko bread crumbs**
½ cup all-purpose flour
2 eggs, lightly beaten
2 cups vegetable oil

1 Wash shrimp with cold water; drain in colander. Blot dry with paper towels.

2 In food processor, mince ginger and green onions. Add water chestnuts; give 2 quick pulses to chop coarsely. Add shrimp, cornstarch, salt, sugar, sherry, Asian sesame oil and egg white to processor; process until shrimp are finely minced. (*Without processor, mince shrimp, ginger, green onions and water chestnuts by hand; mix with all remaining filling ingredients.*)

3 Lightly oil tray, palms and fingers to prevent filling from sticking when forming shrimp balls. Oil both sides of 1-tablespoon measuring spoon. Measure 1 level tablespoon filling. Roll it to form a ball with palms; place on oiled tray. Repeat with remaining filling.

4 Place bread crumbs, flour and eggs in 3 separate bowls. Line tray with parchment paper. Roll each shrimp ball in flour until well coated. Place ball in egg; coat evenly. Drain from egg mixture; transfer to bread crumbs. Using tablespoon, roll ball until coated with crumbs; place on tray. Repeat with remaining filling and coating. With clean hands, lightly shape each into a round ball; place on clean tray.

5 Fill large saucepan ³/4 to 1 inch deep with oil. Heat oil to 325°F. Fry a few balls at a time 1½ minutes or until shrimp turn pink and balls are crisp and golden outside. Drain on paper towels. Repeat with remaining balls. Serve with Sweet and Tangy Sauce.

TIPS *Uncooked shrimp balls can be made up to ½ a day ahead and stored in refrigerator before frying. Although they taste best when freshly fried, fried ones can be refrigerated 3 to 4 days. Reheat after defrosting in a preheated 325°F oven about 15 minutes or until crisp and heated through.

**To make your own bread crumbs, trim crusts from 12 slices of white bread; cut each piece into quarters. In food processor, pulse 8 quarters at a time until bread is coarsely crumbled. Repeat with remaining bread. Spread crumbs on tray; air-dry 1 to 2 days before using. They can be made many days ahead, and stored in an airtight container.

24 shrimp balls.

Crispy Fried Shrimp Balls with Sweet and Tangy Sauce

SWEET AND TANGY SAUCE

While Crispy Fried Shrimp Balls *are delicious solo, they're even tastier when served with this sauce.*

    3   tablespoons vegetable oil
 1 1/2 tablespoons minced fresh ginger
    5   tablespoons minced green onions
    1   cup water
  1/2   cup ketchup
  1/4   cup soy sauce
  1/4   cup plus 2 teaspoons sugar or to taste
    2   teaspoons cornstarch stirred into 4 teaspoons water
    1   tablespoon Asian sesame oil (optional)

1 In small saucepan, heat oil over medium-high heat until hot. Add ginger and 4 tablespoons of the green onions; sauté 30 seconds. Add water, ketchup, soy sauce and sugar; bring to a boil, stirring constantly, until well mixed. Slowly, stir cornstarch mixture into sauce, stirring constantly, until sauce is thickened. Stir in sesame oil; remove from heat. Just before serving, sprinkle with remaining tablespoon green onion.

1 3/4 cups.

STIR-FRIED CHICKEN WITH PEANUTS

For best results, do not overcook the chicken and vegetables. This dish is at its best served immediately after cooking. For those who prefer milder fare, this dish is equally delicious without crushed red pepper.

MARINADE
 4 teaspoons cornstarch
 1 teaspoon salt
 2 tablespoons dry sherry

CHICKEN
 1 1/2 lb. boneless skinless chicken breast, cubed (1 1/2 inch)

SAUCE
 4 teaspoons sugar
 1 tablespoon cornstarch
 3 tablespoons water
 2 tablespoons dry sherry
 1/4 cup plus 2 tablespoons soy sauce or to taste
 2 teaspoons wine vinegar

STIR-FRY

6 tablespoons vegetable oil
2 cups red bell peppers, chopped into bite-size pieces
2 cups snow peas, stringed, chopped into bite-size pieces
1 cup sliced water chestnuts
1 1/2 teaspoons crushed red pepper or to taste*
2 tablespoons minced fresh ginger
2 tablespoons minced fresh garlic
4 green onions, cut into 1/2-inch pieces
1 cup unsalted dry-roasted peanuts, chopped

1 In large bowl, stir together 4 teaspoons cornstarch, 1 teaspoon salt and 2 tablespoons dry sherry; add chicken, stirring to coat.

2 In medium bowl, stir together sugar, 1 tablespoon cornstarch, water, 2 tablespoons dry sherry, soy sauce and wine vinegar.

3 Heat wok or large skillet over high heat until very hot. Heat 2 tablespoons of the oil until hot. Stir-fry 1/2 of the chicken over high heat until no longer pink in center. Remove from wok with slotted spatula; keep warm in 200°F oven. Repeat with 2 tablespoons of the oil and remaining chicken.

4 Cook red bell peppers, snow peas and water chestnuts in oil remaining in wok about 1 minute or until crisp-tender. (*Add additional oil if needed.*) Remove from wok.

5 Rinse and dry wok. Heat remaining 2 tablespoons oil in wok over medium heat. Fry crushed red pepper about 30 seconds. Add ginger and garlic; cook about 1 minute, taking care not to burn garlic. Add green onions; cook about 30 seconds. Increase heat to high; return chicken and vegetables to wok. Stir sauce; add to wok. Cook and stir until sauce is thickened. Sauce should coat chicken and vegetables without being runny. Add peanuts; toss to mix. Serve immediately.

6 servings.

Stir-Fried Chicken with Peanuts

GRILLED EGGPLANTS WITH BASIL

This is an easy dish and can be made ahead. Asian eggplants are long and slim, about 6 to 10 inches long and 2 inches thick, with a purple color. They have a thin skin with almost no seeds or bitter taste, so they are preferred in this dish. Look for firm, unblemished eggplants in Asian markets almost year-round.

SAUCE

3 tablespoons water
2 tablespoons rice vinegar
3 tablespoons fish sauce* or to
   taste
2 tablespoons sugar or to taste
1½ tablespoons minced fresh
   garlic
½ teaspoon crushed red pepper
   or to taste
4 tablespoons shredded fresh
   Thai or sweet basil**

EGGPLANT

1½ lb. Asian eggplants or small
   Italian eggplant
½ red bell pepper
2 tablespoons vegetable oil
2 tablespoons coarsely chopped
   fresh coriander

1 In small saucepan, heat
   water, vinegar, fish sauce
   and sugar until sugar is
   dissolved. Add garlic,
   crushed red pepper and
   basil; return to a boil.
   Quickly remove from heat.

2 Remove stems from
   eggplants. Cut crosswise
   into 2- to 3-inch long
   sections; cut each section
   into 4 or 6 wedges
   depending on diameter of
   eggplant. (*Wedges cook
   more evenly when cut into
   similar sizes.*) Cut bell
   pepper into 2x⅛-inch
   shreds.

Grilled Eggplants with Basil

3   Heat charcoal grill, grill pan or broiler until very hot. Brush both sides of eggplant wedges with oil. Grill eggplants on both sides until just soft but still firm, about 5 minutes depending on eggplant size and heat level. Place grilled eggplant in bowl; toss with sauce until evenly coated. Add bell pepper; toss to mix. Eggplants can be made ahead and served at room temperature. Just before serving, sprinkle with coriander.

> TIPS *Look for fish sauce, used throughout Southeast Asia in much the same way as soy sauce, in the Asian section of supermarkets.
>
> **Thai basil is available at Asian Markets.

6 servings.

HOME STYLE FRIED RICE

It is important to use cold, firm, precooked long-grain rice to get light, fluffy fried rice.

4 tablespoons vegetable oil
2 eggs, beaten with 1/4 teaspoon salt
1 cup diced fresh snow peas (1/4 inch)
1 cup diced orange or red bell pepper (1/4 inch)
1/4 teaspoon salt or to taste
2 green onions, chopped
4 cups cold cooked rice
1 cup diced boiled ham (1/4 inch)
2 tablespoons soy sauce or to taste

1   Heat wok or large skillet until hot; heat 1 tablespoon of the oil. Stir in eggs; scramble until set. Remove from wok. Heat 1 tablespoon of the oil; stir-fry snow peas, bell pepper and 1/4 teaspoon salt about 1 minute. Remove vegetables from wok.

2   Heat remaining 2 tablespoons oil in wok; stir-fry green onions 30 seconds. Add rice; toss to coat with oil. Stir in ham. Add soy sauce; stir to coat rice. Return vegetables and eggs to wok. Break up eggs with spatula. Stir and cook until ingredients are heated through. Season to taste; serve hot.

6 servings.

MELONS IN MINT AND GINGER INFUSION

Asian cooks are not renowned for their pastries and cakes; they usually end meals with fresh fruit. This recipe will make a light and refreshing ending. If desired, serve with your favorite cookies.

FRUIT
6 cups assorted melon balls or 3/4-inch cubes (cantaloupe, Honeydew and watermelon)
2 cups cubed pineapple (3/4 inch thick)

INFUSION
1 1/2 cups water
1 cup sugar
1/4 teaspoon salt
12 slices ginger, peeled, sliced 1/8x1x1-inch
1 1/2 cups packed fresh mint (about 100 leaves)

1   In large bowl, combine fruit; cover and refrigerate.

2   In medium saucepan, heat water, sugar, salt and ginger to boiling over high heat. Reduce heat; simmer, covered, 6 minutes. Stir in mint until leaves are wilted; remove from heat. Cool to room temperature; store in refrigerator, covered, 2 hours. Before serving, strain infusion; toss with chilled fruit. Serve fruit in long stem glasses or bowls. Spoon additional ginger infusion over fruit; garnish with mint sprigs.

6 servings.

*Melons in Mint
and Ginger Infusion*

TASTES OF GREECE

Michele Anna Jordan

In Greece, you see many of the same ingredients as you do throughout the western Mediterranean region — especially olive oil, lemon and seafood. You also begin to notice influences from the Middle East and North Africa, such as yogurt, oranges, pistachios and bulgur. Of course, there are Greece's unique contributions, too: bay leaves and salty feta cheese. These are the elements that make the best of Greek food so exciting, creating an interplay of texture and temperature, a contrast of tastes and aromas.

You can echo many of these elements in table decorations, from big bowls of lemons and oranges to branches of olive and bay trees, if you have them.

This menu is indulgent, with its swordfish and prawns together in a single dish. Perfect for a celebration feast!

SHRIMP AND HERBS | BULGUR PILAF AND GRILLED ZUCCHINI WITH CUCUMBER-YOGURT SAUCE | RICE PUDDING WITH ORANGES AND PISTACHIO

STUFFED GRAPE LEAVES

There are many different kinds of dolmathes, or stuffed grape leaves: some are filled with rice, pine nuts and currants; others with lamb and raisins. This is a tangy version that includes both rice and lamb, along with plenty of fresh lemon juice.

1 lb. lean ground lamb	1 cup tomato sauce
4 garlic cloves, minced	1/2 cup extra-virgin olive oil
1 tablespoon minced fresh oregano	Juice of 3 lemons
Grated peel of 1 lemon	1 jar grape leaves (about 30 to 40)
1/8 teaspoon kosher (coarse) salt	1 cup boiling water
1/8 teaspoon freshly ground pepper	Lemon wedges
1/2 cup cooked long-grain white rice	

Stuffed Grape Leaves

1   In medium skillet, sauté lamb over medium-low heat, using fork to break it up. Cook, stirring with fork frequently, until lamb just loses its pink color and releases most of its fat. Drain off all but 2 teaspoons of fat; return to heat. Add garlic, 2 teaspoons of the oregano and lemon peel; season with salt and pepper. Stir in rice. Remove from heat; cool until mixture is easy to handle.

2   In small saucepan, stir together tomato sauce, olive oil and lemon juice over medium heat. Stir in remaining teaspoon oregano; simmer 3 minutes. Season with salt and generous amount of pepper; remove from heat.

3   Line heavy, wide saucepan with single layer of grape leaves.

4   To fill remaining leaves, set 1 leaf, dull side up, on work surface; place 2 tablespoons filling in center. Fold stem end of leaf over filling; fold in 2 sides. Roll bundle toward leaf tip. Place filled leaf, seam side down, in saucepan. Continue until all grape leaves have been filled, making a second layer if needed. Pour boiling water and sauce over grape leaves; set heat-proof plate on top of leaves to weight them. Bring to a boil over medium heat. Reduce heat to low; cover. Simmer 40 minutes; remove from heat. Uncover; remove weight. Cool 10 to 15 minutes. Carefully transfer filled leaves to platter; season with pepper. Garnish with lemon wedges; serve immediately.

6 servings.

FETA AND OLIVES MARINATED IN OLIVE OIL, LEMON AND BAY

Feta cheese is good enough on its own, and is often part of a Greek appetizer platter. Here, it is perfumed with lemon and bay, two classic flavors of Greek cuisine.

   1   bay leaf
   8   oz. Greek feta, cut into 3/8-inch thick wedges
   6   oz. olives such as kalamata or picholine
       Grated peel of 1 lemon
       Juice of 1 lemon (about 3 tablespoons)
 1/8   teaspoon freshly ground pepper
 1/3   cup extra-virgin olive oil

1   Several hours before serving, put bay leaf in bottom of medium serving bowl; add feta and olives. Scatter lemon peel on top; pour lemon juice over cheese and olives. Season with pepper. Drizzle with oil; cover. Refrigerate. Remove from refrigerator 30 minutes before serving. Serve with warm pita or country-style bread.

6 servings.

Marinated and Grilled Swordfish Steaks with Shrimp and Herbs

MARINATED AND GRILLED SWORDFISH STEAKS WITH SHRIMP AND HERBS

If you don't have swordfish, you can use shark or ahi tuna instead. If using tuna, reduce the cooking time to about 5 minutes; fresh tuna should always be served rare.

6	(6- to 8-oz.) swordfish steaks
3/4	lb. shelled, deveined uncooked large shrimp, tails on
1/8	teaspoon kosher (coarse) salt
1/8	teaspoon freshly ground pepper
	Grated peel of 2 lemons
	Juice of 2 lemons
1/3	cup olive oil
3	garlic cloves, minced
1	tablespoon minced fresh Italian parsley
1	tablespoon minced fresh Greek oregano
2	teaspoons minced fresh thyme
	Olive oil
2 to 3	tablespoons extra-virgin olive oil
	Fresh herb sprigs
1	lemon, cut in wedges

1 Place swordfish in single layer in Pyrex baking dish. Sprinkle with shrimp. Season both sides with salt and pepper. In small bowl, mix together lemon peel, lemon juice, 1/3 cup olive oil, garlic, parsley, oregano and thyme. Season with salt and pepper; pour over seafood. Turn swordfish to coat thoroughly. Cover; refrigerate 3 hours. Bring to room temperature before grilling.

2 To prepare swordfish, heat charcoal or stove-top grill. Brush or shake off excess marinade; grill fish, turning once, until just cooked through, about 10 minutes for 1-inch thick steaks. Transfer to individual plates; keep warm.

3 In wok or small skillet, heat a very small amount of olive oil over high heat until hot. Sauté shrimp about 1 1/2 minutes until they just turn pink. Season with salt and pepper. Spoon shrimp over swordfish. Drizzle with extra-virgin olive oil. Garnish with herb sprigs and lemon wedges. Serve immediately.

6 servings.

BULGUR PILAF AND GRILLED ZUCCHINI WITH CUCUMBER-YOGURT SAUCE

Although this dish is outstanding as part of a larger feast, it is also excellent on its own for a light and quick vegetarian meal.

1	cucumber, peeled
2	teaspoons kosher (coarse) salt, plus more for seasoning
2	cups plain yogurt, preferably Russian-style
2	tablespoons minced fresh chives
4 to 6	garlic cloves, minced
3	tablespoons olive oil
1	small yellow onion, diced
1	cup medium or large grain bulgur
2	cups hot vegetable or chicken broth or stock
1	tablespoon minced fresh Italian parsley
2	teaspoons minced fresh Greek oregano
1/8	teaspoon freshly ground pepper
6	medium zucchini, trimmed, halved lengthwise
	Olive oil for zucchini
1	lemon, halved

1 Cut cucumber in quarters lengthwise; remove seeds using small knife. Cut cucumber into small dice; place in medium bowl. Toss with 2 teaspoons salt. Let sit 20 minutes. Transfer to strainer; press out as much moisture as possible. Return to bowl. Stir in yogurt, chives and garlic. Cover; set aside.

2 In medium saucepan, heat 3 tablespoons olive oil over medium-low heat. Add onion; sauté about 7 to 8 minutes or until tender and fragrant. Add bulgur; stir 1 to 2 minutes. Stir in broth, parsley and oregano; season with salt and pepper. Reduce heat to low; cook 20 minutes. Remove from heat (do not lift lid); let rest 15 minutes. Fluff with fork.

3 Place zucchini in wide bowl; drizzle with small amount of olive oil, turning zucchini gently to coat. Season with salt and pepper. Grill, cut side down, over charcoal fire or on stove-top grill heated to medium until evenly marked and just becoming tender. Turn zucchini; grill an additional 3 to 4 minutes. Transfer to serving plate; squeeze juice of 1/2 of the lemon over it. Season with salt and pepper. Cut remaining lemon 1/2 in wedges; use to garnish plate. Transfer bulgur to serving bowl; serve alongside zucchini.

6 servings.

RICE PUDDING WITH ORANGES AND PISTACHIO

Everyone loves rice pudding, perhaps the most comforting of all desserts. For an even richer version, use coconut milk in place of heavy cream.

3 cups whole milk
1 (2-inch) piece vanilla bean
2/3 cup Arborio or other
    short-grain rice, rinsed in
    cool water
    Grated peel of 2 oranges
1/3 cup sugar
    Dash kosher (coarse) salt
2 tablespoons butter
1 egg
2 egg yolks
    Juice of 2 oranges, strained
1/2 cup heavy cream, lightly
    beaten
1/4 cup minced pistachios
2 tablespoons whole shelled
    pistachios
    Orange wedges

Rice Pudding with Oranges and Pistachio

1 In medium saucepan, heat milk and vanilla bean over medium heat until boiling. Stir in rice, orange peel, sugar and salt; reduce heat to low. Simmer slowly 45 to 60 minutes or until mixture is thick and creamy. Stir in butter; remove from heat.

2 Heat oven to 350°F.

3 In bowl, beat egg and egg yolks until they are pale yellow; whisk in orange juice until well mixed. Whisk in cream.

4 Remove vanilla bean from rice with tongs. Fold egg mixture into rice using rubber spatula. Fold in minced pistachios. Spoon batter into 6 custard cups or ramekins; place custard cups into ovenproof pan; place in oven. Pour hot water into pan so that it comes halfway up sides of cups. Bake 20 to 25 minutes or until just barely set.

5 Remove from oven; cool 15 to 30 minutes. Place each custard cup on small serving plate; garnish with whole pistachios and orange wedges. Serve warm. Store in refrigerator.

6 servings.

MEAL FROM INDIA

Raghavan Iyer

CHANA DAL SHORBA | MUCHEE CHETTINAD | BHARELA BAINGAN

he hearty first course soup, Chana Dal Shorba, *is delicious either hot or cold, making it an ideal introduction to an Indian meal during the cool winter months or the dogs days of summer.*

The chettinad style of cooking from the southern region of India elegantly combines fiery peppercorns, chiles and coconut milk with the ocean's bountiful harvest to create a taste sensation that is unparalleled in the universe. Use any firm fish filets of your choice for the Muchee Chettinad.

Bharela Baingan *is often served as an accompaniment on special occasions. During weddings in northern India, whole eggplants are dropped directly onto hot coals in clay-lined ovens called tandoors, skin charred black, and later peeled to unveil the smoky-rich, grainy pulp. This smoky pulp is mashed and flavored with fresh ground spices and served with hot clay-oven baked breads (naans) and rice pilafs (biryanis).*

When you marry two classics — one from northern India (saffron) and the other from southern United States (black-eyed peas) — the symbiotic relationship will draw accolades from millions. Serve Zarda Pulao *as an accompaniment to your main course or offer it as a humble meal with plain yogurt.*

Finally, an Indian meal is never complete without appeasing the sweet tooth at the dinner table. And if you mention dessert, chances are that cardamom will make its presence known. Elaichi Ice Cream *is suprisingly rich and complex tasting.*

ZARDA PULAO | ELAICHI ICE CREAM

CHANA DAL SHORBA

YELLOW SPLIT PEA SOUP WITH CHILE-SPIKED CARAMELIZED ONIONS

I always enjoy this soup with a thick slice of freshly baked French bread for a meal all on its own.

1	cup yellow split peas, sorted, rinsed
4 1/2	cups water
1	medium tomato, coarsely chopped
4	medium garlic cloves, coarsely chopped
2	tablespoons vegetable oil
1	teaspoon cumin seeds
1	medium red onion, thinly sliced
2	serrano chiles, coarsely chopped
1	teaspoon salt
1/2	teaspoon ground turmeric
1	cup plain yogurt, whisked
2	tablespoons finely chopped fresh cilantro

1 In 2-quart saucepan, bring split peas and 4 cups of the water to a boil over medium-high heat; skim off and discard any foam that forms on surface. Stir in tomato and garlic; reduce heat. Simmer partially covered, stirring occasionally, about 25 minutes or until peas are tender.

2 Meanwhile, in medium skillet, heat oil over medium-high heat until hot. Add cumin seeds; sizzle about 10 seconds or until seeds are reddish brown. Add onion and chiles; stir-fry about 5 minutes or until onion turns caramel brown. Stir in salt, turmeric and remaining 1/2 cup water. Scrape contents of skillet into saucepan with cooked peas.

3 Continue simmering peas partially covered, stirring occasionally, an additional 5 minutes to blend flavors. Cool peas 15 to 20 minutes. Transfer to blender; puree until smooth. Return pureed soup to saucepan. Fold in yogurt; serve soup sprinkled with cilantro.

4 servings.

Chana Dal Shorba

Muchee Chettinad

MUCHEE CHETTINAD

GRILLED SALMON WITH MUSTARD SEED-FLAVORED CRÈME FRAÎCHE

You can also use this combination of flavors as a marinade for boneless, skinless chicken breasts. Crème fraîche is widely available in the dairy section of large supermarkets. If unavailable, you can make your own by stirring 1 tablespoon sour cream into 1 cup heavy whipping cream. Let the mixture sit at room temperature (preferably in a warm, humid spot) for about 2 hours or until the mixture sets to a yogurt-like consistency.

1   teaspoon cumin seeds
1/2 teaspoon black peppercorns
1   (3-inch) cinnamon stick, broken into smaller pieces
1/2 cup coconut milk
1   teaspoon salt
2   tablespoons finely chopped fresh cilantro
4   (6-oz.) boneless skinless salmon fillets
1   tablespoon vegetable oil
1   teaspoon black or yellow mustard seeds
1   serrano chile, finely chopped
1   cup crème fraîche

1   Heat small skillet over medium-high heat. Add cumin, peppercorns and cinnamon; toast spices about 1 minute or until cumin seeds turn reddish brown, peppercorns crackle and spices turn fragrant. Transfer spice mixture to coffee grinder; grind until mixture resembles texture of finely ground black pepper.

2   In medium bowl, combine ground spices, coconut milk, salt and 1 tablespoon of the cilantro. Coat salmon fillets with marinade; refrigerate 1 to 6 hours.

3   Meanwhile in same skillet, heat oil over medium-high heat until hot. Add mustard seeds. Once seeds start to pop, cover skillet and wait until seeds stop popping. Remove skillet from heat; sauté chile and remaining tablespoon cilantro in hot oil. Pour oil mixture over crème fraîche; mix well. Keep chilled.

4   Brush grill rack with vegetable oil. Heat coals or gas grill for direct heat. Cover; grill fish 5 to 6 inches from medium-high heat 6 to 10 minutes, turning once, until fish flakes easily with a fork. To broil, heat broiler. Place fish on rack in broiler pan. Broil with tops 2 to 3 inches from heat 6 to 10 minutes, turning once, until fish flakes easily with a fork. Serve with sauce.

4 servings.

BHARELA BAINGAN

SPICED EGGPLANT PÂTÉ IN "BOATS"

These delectable "boats" are more than just edible; they also make a great presence on the dinner plate.

2   small eggplants (about 1 lb. each)
2   tablespoons vegetable oil
1   medium onion, coarsely chopped
4   medium garlic cloves, coarsely chopped
1   teaspoon cumin seeds, ground
1   tablespoon coriander seeds, ground
1   teaspoon salt
1/2   teaspoon cayenne pepper
1/4   teaspoon ground turmeric
1/2   cup water
1   large tomato, finely chopped
2   tablespoons finely chopped fresh cilantro

1   Heat oven to 350°F. Lightly grease ovenproof baking dish.

2   Trim eggplants; cut lengthwise. Scoop out as much pulp as possible with melon baller or spoon, without tearing through skin. Place eggplant pulp in medium bowl.

3   In wok or deep skillet, heat oil over medium-high heat until hot. Add onion, and garlic; stir-fry 4 to 5 minutes or until caramel brown. Stir in eggplant pulp, cumin, coriander, salt, cayenne pepper and turmeric; stir-fry about 1 minute. Pour in water. Reduce heat to medium; cover wok. Cook, stirring occasionally, 7 to 9 minutes or until eggplant is tender. Cool. Transfer mixture to food processor; process until smooth.

4   Transfer pâté to medium bowl; fold in tomato and 1 tablespoon of the cilantro. Divide and spread pâté into scooped-out eggplant boats.

5   Place boats in prepared baking dish; bake uncovered 35 to 40 minutes or until center is warmed through and boats are tender to the touch.

6   Serve sprinkled with remaining tablespoon cilantro.

4 servings.

Bharela Baingan

ZARDA PULAO

BASMATI RICE WITH SAFFRON AND BLACK-EYED PEAS

Saffron is unarguably the world's most expensive spice. These stamens from the crocus blossom are hand-picked and often thousands of blossoms sacrifice their stamens to produce an ounce of pure saffron. Their flavors are hauntingly rich and delicate at the same time ... just a few threads can permeate an entire dish. Refrain from purchasing saffron powder, as it may not be in its pure state.

1	cup basmati or long-grain rice
2	tablespoons canola or vegetable oil
2	(3-inch) cinnamon sticks
2	bay leaves
1	medium red onion, halved, thinly sliced
1	(15- to 16-oz.) can black-eyed peas, drained, rinsed
1½	teaspoons salt
1	teaspoon garam masala
½	teaspoon saffron threads
2	cups cold water
¼	cup finely chopped fresh basil

Zarda Pulao

1 Place rice in medium bowl; add enough water to cover by about 1 inch. With fingertips, gently swish grains until water becomes cloudy; drain. Repeat 3 or 4 times until water remains almost clear. Cover with cold water; soak 20 to 30 minutes. Drain.

2 In heavy 2-quart saucepan, heat oil over medium-high heat until hot. Add cinnamon sticks and bay leaves; sizzle 15 to 20 seconds or until cinnamon sticks swell up. Immediately add onion; stir-fry 2 to 3 minutes or until partially brown.

3 Stir in black-eyed peas, salt and garam masala. Add rice and saffron; gently stir-fry 1 minute, taking care not to break up tender grains of rice. Pour in cold water. Bring to a boil, stirring once. Once almost all of the water evaporates, cover pan with well-fitted lid; reduce heat to lowest setting. Cook an additional 5 minutes. Turn off burner; let sit undisturbed at least 5 to 10 minutes.

4 Remove cover; fluff rice with fork or spoon to release steam. Sprinkle with basil.

4 to 6 servings.

ELAICHI ICE CREAM

CARDAMOM ICE CREAM WITH MANGOES AND PAPAYA

This ice cream is surprisingly rich and complex tasting, given that it has only six ingredients. Which goes to further show that simple is often spectacular.

8	cups whole milk
1/2	cup fat-free cholesterol-free egg product
1/2	cup sugar
1/2	teaspoon cardamom seeds, ground
1	large mango, peeled, seeded, sliced
1	medium papaya, peeled, seeded, sliced

1 In large, wide-rimmed saucepan or Dutch oven, bring milk to a boil over medium-high heat, stirring constantly to prevent scorching. Continue reducing milk down, 50 to 60 minutes, stirring occasionally and scraping sides of pan to release collected milk solids, until milk is reduced to 2 cups.

2 Cool reduced milk; refrigerate, covered, at least 2 hours or until well chilled.

3 In large bowl, beat together egg product and sugar with electric mixer on medium speed, scraping bowl constantly, until batter is smooth and creamy yellow.

4 Add reduced milk and cardamom; continue beating 2 to 3 minutes until well blended.

5 Transfer batter to ice cream maker; freeze according to manufacturer's instructions.

6 Serve ice cream over sliced mango and papaya.

About 1 quart.

FLAVORS OF MEXICO

Lisa Golden Schroeder

Capture the vibrant flavors of Mexico in a contemporary menu that features one of the famous Aztec mole sauces, considered celebration food in every part of Mexico. Variations abound in each region of the country, but moles are basically thick, complex sauces made of dried chiles, nuts, seeds, flavoring vegetables, spices (and sometimes unsweetened chocolate, as in the famous mole poblano). Mole sauces can be purchased in jars in Mexican markets, but those renditions can't touch the taste of a freshly made, slowly simmered homemade mole.

A creamy golden soup begins this party, visually appealing with a garnish of spiced green pumpkin seeds. A red chile mole follows, rich with peanuts and pork. Serve with hot steamed rice or warm corn tortillas to soak up the flavorful sauce. Oven-roasted calabacitas, *a dish of native vegetables with toasted cumin and lime, accompanies the entree. Pretty glazed shortbread wedges filled with pine nuts conclude this special meal, requiring only small cups of sweet Mexican coffee.*

ROASTED CALABACITAS WITH WARM CUMIN VINAIGRETTE   PINE NUT SHORTBREAD WITH ANISE GLAZE

PUMPKIN SOUP WITH SPICED PEPITAS

Pepitas, the hulled green seeds of pumpkins, have been eaten in Mexico since ancient times. A great variety of green and tan pumpkins, as well as other large squash, are native to Mexico and have been an important part of the Mexican diet. This creamy soup is a great do-ahead dish for entertaining and can be made up to 2 days in advance. It also freezes well for longer storage. Look for hulled pumpkin seeds at health food stores, co-ops or a Mexican market.

SOUP

6 cups (about 2 lb.) peeled cubed pumpkin or butternut squash
2 (14.5-oz.) cans chicken broth
1 teaspoon salt
1/2 teaspoon freshly ground pepper
1 cup half-and-half
1 tablespoon butter or margarine
2 teaspoons grated orange peel

SPICED PEPITAS

1 tablespoon butter or margarine
1 cup hulled pumpkin seeds (pepitas)
3/4 teaspoon chili powder
1/2 teaspoon garlic salt
1/8 teaspoon cayenne pepper

1 In Dutch oven or large stockpot, combine pumpkin, broth, salt and pepper. Bring to a boil; reduce heat to low. Cover; simmer 20 to 25 minutes or until pumpkin is very tender.

2 Puree pumpkin mixture in food processor or with an immersion blender until smooth. Stir in half-and-half, 1 tablespoon butter and orange peel.

3 Meanwhile, in skillet, melt 1 tablespoon butter over medium heat. Sauté pumpkin seeds with chili powder, garlic salt and cayenne pepper until fragrant and well coated.

4 Serve soup hot, sprinkled with spiced pepitas.

6 to 8 servings.

Pumpkin Soup with Spiced Pepitas

SMOKY PEANUT PORK MOLE

This fragrant mole sauce is excellent made ahead — not only does it make entertaining easier, but the flavors only get better with time. Served here with roasted pork, the sauce is equally good with grilled chicken or beef, or roasted turkey (which may have been the original meat simmered in Pueblan mole poblano). Ancho chiles are ripened and dried poblano chiles. Other dried chiles can be used to vary the heat and flavor of the dish.

MOLE SAUCE

3 dried ancho chiles
4 ripe plum tomatoes
2 tablespoons olive oil
1 small white onion, chopped
3 garlic cloves, chopped
1 cup dry-roasted peanuts
2 (6-inch) corn tortillas, torn into
  pieces
3 canned chipotle chiles en adobo
3/4 teaspoon ground cinnamon
1/2 teaspoon ground cumin
1/4 teaspoon ground allspice
4 cups chicken broth

2 bay leaves
2 tablespoons honey
3/4 to 1 teaspoon salt

PORK

2 1/2 lb. pork loin roast or pork
  tenderloin
1 tablespoon olive oil
6 garlic cloves, crushed
Salt and freshly ground pepper to
  taste

GARNISH

Chopped dry-roasted peanuts

Smoky Peanut Pork Mole

1 Heat oven to 250°F. Toast chiles on baking sheet 3 to 4 minutes or just until fragrant; cool. Remove stems and seeds; tear into pieces. Place in small bowl. Cover with boiling water; soak 30 minutes. Heat broiler.

2 Heat broiler. Place tomatoes on baking sheet; broil 5 minutes or until charred. Turn over and broil other side; cool.

3 In medium skillet, heat 1 tablespoon of the oil over medium-high heat until hot. Add onion and chopped garlic; sauté about 4 minutes or until golden brown. Scrape mixture into food processor. Drain and add rehydrated chiles. Peel tomatoes; add to food processor with juices.

4 Add peanuts, tortillas, chipotles, cinnamon, cumin, allspice and 1 cup of the broth to food processor. Process until smooth, scraping down sides of container as needed.

5 In large, deep skillet, heat remaining tablespoon oil over medium-high heat until very hot. Pour in mixture from food processor, along with 1 cup of the broth. Cook and stir 5 to 8 minutes or until sauce thickens. Stir in remaining 2 cups broth and bay leaves. Reduce heat to low. Partially cover; simmer 30 minutes or until broth mixture is consistency of gravy. Season with honey and salt. Keep warm. (*May be made up to 3 days ahead. Cover and refrigerate.*)

6 To roast pork*, heat oven to 425°F. Rub pork with 1 tablespoon oil and crushed garlic; place in roasting pan. Bake 15 to 20 minutes per pound or until internal temperature reaches 145° to 150°F. (*Bake 18 to 20 minutes for tenderloins.*) Let pork rest 10 minutes, tented with aluminum foil.

7 Thinly slice pork; serve with warm mole sauce, sprinkled with chopped peanuts.

TIP *As an alternative, pork may be grilled over medium-high heat until desired doneness.

6 to 8 servings.

ROASTED CALABACITAS WITH WARM CUMIN VINAIGRETTE

This dish is like a Mexican succotash, filled with native vegetables oven-roasted to concentrate their rich, sweet flavors. Chayote squash (sometimes known as mirliton in the southern United States) are often part of this type of vegetable mixture — they are pear-shaped and pale green, with a mild zucchini-like flavor.

ROASTED VEGETABLES

4 plum tomatoes, halved
2 large zucchini, halved lengthwise
2 ears corn, husk and silk removed
2 large Anaheim chiles, halved
1 red or orange bell pepper, halved
1 small white onion, halved
1 jalapeño or serrano chile, halved

1 tablespoon olive oil
Salt and freshly ground pepper

DRESSING

2 tablespoons lime juice
1 tablespoon olive oil
1/2 teaspoon cumin seeds, toasted*, crushed
Fresh cilantro leaves

1 Heat oven to 450°F. Line 2 large, rimmed baking sheets with aluminum foil; lightly brush foil with oil. Arrange vegetables on baking sheets. Drizzle with 1 tablespoon oil; season with salt and pepper. Bake vegetables 20 to 25 minutes or until very tender and browned, turning occasionally.

2 Cool vegetables 5 minutes. Coarsely chop zucchini and onion; place in large bowl. Remove skin from tomatoes; chop. Slice corn from cobs. Remove charred skin, stems and seeds from bell pepper and chiles; chop. Place all vegetables in large bowl; gently stir together.

3 In small saucepan, whisk lime juice, 1 tablespoon oil and cumin together over medium heat until warm. Pour over vegetables; toss to coat. Sprinkle with cilantro.

> **TIP** *To toast cumin seeds: In skillet, stir seeds over medium-heat until brown and aromatic, about 3 minutes.

6 to 8 servings.

Roasted Calabacitas with Warm Cumin Vinaigrette

PINE NUT SHORTBREAD WITH ANISE GLAZE

Sweet and crumbly with pine nuts, brown sugar and butter, these shortbread wedges are perfect with a cup of dark coffee or used to garnish a dish of dulce de leche ice cream. Pine nuts, which are still laboriously gathered by hand, are tender and easy to chop — toast them in a dry skillet until golden brown before using. Look for Mexican vanilla and unrefined piloncillo sugar (shaped into hard cones) in a Mexican market. To chop the piloncillo sugar, use a serrated knife or process in a food processor.

SHORTBREAD
1 cup butter, softened
3/4 cup packed brown sugar or piloncillo
1 teaspoon Mexican vanilla
2 cups all-purpose flour
1/4 cup finely chopped toasted pine nuts
1/4 teaspoon salt
1/4 cup coarsely chopped toasted pine nuts

GLAZE
1/3 cup powdered sugar
1/4 teaspoon crushed anise seeds
2 teaspoons milk

1   Heat oven to 325°F. In large bowl, beat butter, brown sugar and vanilla together with electric mixer on medium-high speed 3 to 4 minutes or until fluffy. Stir in flour, finely chopped pine nuts and salt; mix well.

2   Press dough evenly into 9-inch fluted tart pan with removable bottom; prick all over with tines of fork. Sprinkle with coarsely chopped pine nuts; press lightly into dough.

3   Bake 45 to 50 minutes or until edges are firm but center is still soft. Cool completely on wire rack. Remove rim from tart pan; cut shortbread into wedges.

4   In small bowl, combine sugar, anise seeds and milk; mix well. Drizzle glaze over shortbread.

6 to 8 servings.

CLASSIC FRANCE

Mary Evans

rance is a country that is passionate about food and eating. The French take time to enjoy their meals, and each other, when gathering together. This menu takes full advantage of that, featuring great ingredients in a delectable way. Each course balances the next. Warm soup is followed by crisp salad. Succulent salmon is enriched with a buttery sauce and enhanced by a simply prepared rice pilaf. Then, instead of a more traditional dark chocolate mousse, close with creamy white chocolate swirled with strawberry puree.

SALMON FILLETS WITH TARRAGON MUSTARD BEURRE BLANC | LEMON RICE TIMBALES | STRAWBERRY-WHITE CHOCOLATE MOUSSE

ASPARAGUS AND MUSHROOM SOUP PRINTANIER

Printanier means spring, and the ingredients in this soup couldn't be more seasonal. By using dried morels instead of fresh, the broth has even more depth and the soup can be made for a longer period of time than the very short season for fresh morels.

1 quart reduced-sodium chicken broth
1 oz. dried morel mushrooms or other dried wild mushrooms
1 cup fresh shelled or frozen peas
1/4 lb. fresh asparagus, trimmed, cut in 2-inch pieces (about 1 cup)
1 small yellow squash, diced (about 1 cup)
1 small leek (white parts only), trimmed, cut in thin, 2-inch long strips (about 1/2 cup)
1/8 teaspoon freshly ground pepper

1 In large saucepan, heat 2 cups of the broth over medium heat until boiling. Place mushrooms in medium bowl; pour boiling broth over mushrooms. Let soak 30 minutes.

2 Place peas, asparagus, yellow squash, leek and pepper in same saucepan; add remaining 2 cups broth. Remove mushrooms with slotted spoon from soaking liquid; cut in halves or quarters depending on size; add to saucepan. Strain soaking liquid through coffee filter; add to saucepan. Bring to a simmer over medium heat; reduce heat to low. Cook 6 to 8 minutes or until vegetables are crisp-tender.

6 servings.

Asparagus and Mushroom Soup Printanier

SEASONAL GREENS WITH ROASTED ONION VINAIGRETTE

Sherry wine vinegar accentuates the nutty flavor of the vinaigrette. If unavailable, substitute red or white wine vinegar.

1	bunch green onions
1	tablespoon plus 6 tablespoons vegetable oil
2	tablespoons sherry wine vinegar
1	teaspoon Dijon mustard
1/4	teaspoon salt
1/8	teaspoon freshly ground pepper
8	cups mixed greens
1/2	cup coarsely chopped toasted hazelnuts*

1   Heat oven to 500°F. Quarter and trim green onions, leaving tender green portion; toss with 1 tablespoon of the oil in shallow baking pan. Bake 10 to 12 minutes or until slightly charred. Let cool; chop.

2   In medium bowl, whisk together vinegar and mustard. Slowly whisk in remaining 6 tablespoons oil; add salt, pepper and chopped roasted onions. Just before serving, toss with greens and hazelnuts.

> TIP *To toast hazelnuts, spread on baking sheet; bake in 375°F oven about 10 minutes or until lightly browned. Cool.

6 servings.

SALMON FILLETS WITH TARRAGON MUSTARD BEURRE BLANC

Beurre blanc is a classic French sauce made with reduced white wine, shallots and butter. Adding tarragon and mustard gives extra depth.

MARINADE
1/4	cup vegetable oil
2	teaspoons mustard seeds
2	tablespoons dried tarragon

FILLETS
2 1/4 to 2 1/2	lb. salmon fillet, skin removed
1/2	teaspoon salt

BEURRE BLANC
1/4	cup Dijon mustard
3	tablespoons finely chopped fresh tarragon
1/2	cup chilled unsalted butter
2	tablespoons chopped shallots
1	cup white wine

1   In covered, shallow saucepan, heat oil and mustard seeds until seeds pop. Remove from heat; stir in dried tarragon. Cool. Place salmon fillet(s) in shallow glass baking dish; rub both sides with cooled marinade. Refrigerate 1 to 4 hours.

2   Heat oven to 425°F. Sprinkle marinated salmon with salt; place in single layer in shallow baking dish. Bake 15 minutes or until fish flakes easily with a fork.

3   Meanwhile, in small bowl, combine mustard and 2 tablespoons of the chopped tarragon. In large saucepan, melt 1 tablespoon of the butter over medium-low heat. Add shallots; sauté 2 to 3 minutes or until tender. Add wine and remaining tablespoon tarragon; increase heat to high. Boil rapidly until mixture is reduced to about 1 to 2 tablespoons. Remove from heat; whisk in mustard mixture. Whisk in remaining butter by tablespoons, returning pan briefly, if needed, to lowest possible heat until all of the butter is emulsified into a creamy sauce.

6 servings.

Salmon Fillets with Tarragon Mustard Buerre Blanc

LEMON RICE TIMBALES

Timbales *are French molds used to shape everything from desserts to vegetables. Here, custard cups stand in admirably to shape rice into an easily made accompaniment.*

- 3   cups chicken broth
- 1¹/₂ cups long-grain rice (not converted)
- 1   cup diced carrots (about 2 medium)
- 1   tablespoon lemon juice
- 1¹/₂ teaspoons grated lemon peel
- 2   tablespoons finely diced red bell pepper

Lemon Rice Timbales

1   In medium saucepan, heat broth, rice, carrots, lemon juice and lemon peel over medium heat until simmering. Reduce heat to low; cover. Cook 20 minutes or until rice is tender.

2   Meanwhile, sprinkle 1 teaspoon bell pepper in bottom of each of 6 (6-oz.) custard cups. Divide cooked rice among cups, pressing slightly. Let rest 3 to 4 minutes; unmold onto plate.

6 servings.

STRAWBERRY-WHITE CHOCOLATE MOUSSE

Heating the custard base for this mousse to 160°F cooks the yolks and eliminates any raw egg food safety concerns.

     1   pint strawberries
     2   tablespoons plus 1/4 cup sugar
     4   egg yolks
    1/2 cup milk
     6   oz. white chocolate, chopped
    11/2 cups heavy whipping cream

1   Reserve 6 smaller strawberries for garnish. Hull and slice remaining berries in food processor; sprinkle with 2 tablespoons of the sugar. Let rest 10 minutes; pulse to form chunky puree. Set aside.

2   In medium bowl, whisk egg yolks and remaining 1/4 cup sugar. In small saucepan, heat milk over medium heat until bubbles form around edge. Whisk hot milk slowly into egg yolk mixture; return to saucepan. Heat over medium-low heat, stirring constantly, until mixture thickens and reaches 160°F. (*Use instant read thermometer to check.*) Remove from heat; stir in white chocolate. Continue stirring until chocolate has melted. Cool to room temperature.

3   In large mixer bowl, beat whipping cream on medium-high speed until soft peaks form. Reduce speed to low; slowly stir in chocolate mixture. Increase speed to medium-high; beat until mixture forms soft mounds. Do not overmix.

4   Chill 1 hour or serve immediately. To serve, spoon 1/3 cup mousse into first of 6 wine glasses or small glass dishes. Top with 1/6 of pureed strawberries (about 3 tablespoons). Top with 1/3 cup mousse. Repeat with remaining glasses. Garnish each with small strawberry. Store in refrigerator.

6 servings.

ITALIAN DESSERT PARTY

Michele Anna Jordan

TRIO OF ICES | SIMPLE SYRUP | POLENTA CAKE WITH MASCARPONE AND RASPBERRIES

A single dessert might be a rich and luscious indulgence, or a light and refreshing flourish.

A dessert buffet is, by definition, indulgent, though this one attempts to delight the palate, satisfy lingering hunger, and refresh … all at the same time.

From the delicacy of the sorbets and poached pear to the richness of the mascarpone, these desserts will pleasure the senses on every level. You should serve two beverages alongside — strong coffee (such as espresso with a twist of lemon peel) and either grappa or an Italian dessert wine such as vin santo.

PEARS POACHED IN CHIANTI | POLENTA AND HAZELNUT BISCOTTI

TRIO OF ICES

RASPBERRY GRANITA, ESPRESSO GRANITA, LEMON GRANITA

*When you taste the liquid mixture for any frozen dessert, it should be very sweet —
sweeter than you think it should be. Once frozen, the sweetness won't be so intense.*

RASPBERRY GRANITA
    2   cups fresh raspberries or boysenberries
    1   tablespoon framboise or lemon juice
1/3 to 1/2 cup Simple Syrup, plus more to taste (recipe follows)

ESPRESSO GRANITA
    2   cups espresso, chilled
1/4 to 1/3 cup Simple Syrup, plus more to taste (recipe follows)

LEMON GRANITA
    2   cups fresh lemon juice
1/2 to 3/4 cup Simple Syrup, plus more to taste (recipe follows)

1   Place raspberries in wide, shallow bowl; drizzle with framboise. Set aside 30 minutes. Puree in food
    processor; press through medium sieve. Discard seeds. Stir in 1/3 cup syrup. Taste; add more syrup to
    taste. Pour mixture into metal container such as ice cube tray or pie plate. Cover with aluminum foil;
    place on flat surface in freezer 30 minutes. Using fork or small whisk, stir granita, pulling crystals from
    sides into the center, mixing them with the liquid. Cover; return to freezer. Stir every 30 minutes or so
    until mixture is slushy and somewhat stiff. Spoon mixture into lidded container; cover tightly. Return
    to freezer.

2   To make Espresso Granita, combine espresso and 1/4 cup syrup. Taste mixture; add syrup to taste.
    Freeze using method for Raspberry Granita.

3   To make Lemon Granita, combine lemon juice and 1/2 cup syrup. Taste mixture; add syrup to taste.
    Freeze using method for Raspberry Granita.

4   To serve, use small ice cream scoop to make balls of each. Place 1 or 2 scoops of each flavor in dessert
    bowls; return bowls to freezer. Remove just before serving.

6 to 8 servings.

SIMPLE SYRUP

Simple Syrup, *which is also known as bar sugar in reference to its use by bartenders, is used to sweeten sorbets, gelatos, a variety of other desserts, and many beverages.*

4　cups sugar
2　cups water

1　In heavy saucepan, cook sugar and water, without stirring, over high heat until boiling. Reduce heat to medium-low; simmer 4 to 5 minutes or until sugar is dissolved and syrup is completely transparent. Remove from heat; cover. Cool to room temperature. Store, covered, in refrigerator up to 6 weeks.

About 4 cups.

Trio of Ices

POLENTA CAKE WITH MASCARPONE AND RASPBERRIES

Light and delightful best describes this wonderful dessert from heaven.

1	cup buttermilk
3/4	cup polenta
2	cups fresh raspberries
3	tablespoons framboise
	Butter and flour for tube pan
2	cups all-purpose flour
2	teaspoons baking powder
3/4	teaspoon baking soda
1/2	teaspoon kosher (coarse) salt
1	cup unsalted butter, softened
1	cup sugar
2	extra-large eggs, lightly beaten
8	oz. mascarpone cheese*

1 In medium bowl, combine buttermilk and polenta; cover. Set aside 1 hour.

2 In medium bowl, gently toss raspberries with framboise; set aside.

3 Heat oven to 350°F. Coat inside of 9x3-inch tube pan with butter and flour.

4 In large bowl, mix together 2 cups flour, baking powder, baking soda and salt. In another large bowl, cream 1 cup butter and sugar using electric mixer until light and fluffy. Add eggs; beat well.

5 Using rubber spatula, fold in 1/3 of the soaked polenta and 1/3 of the dry ingredients. Repeat, alternating between polenta and dry mixture, until all ingredients have been combined. Pour cake batter in pan; bake 35 to 45 minutes or until lightly browned.

6 Cool in pan 5 minutes. Invert; cool completely on wire rack. Set cooled cake on flat serving plate. In small bowl, whisk mascarpone to loosen it slightly; spoon into cake's center. Spoon raspberries and their juices on top and around cake. To serve, cut wedges of cake; add generous spoonfuls of mascarpone and raspberries to each serving. Serve immediately. Refrigerate leftovers.

TIP *If mascarpone is not available, substitute 1 cup cream cheese mixed with 3 tablespoons whipping cream.

6 to 8 servings.

Polenta Cake with Mascarpone and Raspberries

PEARS POACHED IN CHIANTI

When pears are poached in wine, the fruit lends its flavor to the liquid as the wine flavors the pears. The reduced cooking liquid intensifies these flavors.

Juice of 1 lemon
6 ripe but firm pears
1 (750-ml) bottle Chianti
1 cup sugar
Grated peel of 1 orange
2 (2-inch) cinnamon sticks
4 or 5 whole cloves
2 whole allspice berries
Fresh mint sprigs

1 Fill large bowl 1/2 full with cool water; stir in lemon juice. Peel pears, leaving them whole with stems intact; place each peeled pear in bowl of water before peeling the next one.

2 In medium saucepan, heat Chianti, sugar, orange peel, cinnamon sticks, cloves and allspice over medium heat. Cook, stirring constantly, until boiling and sugar dissolves. Reduce heat to low. Drain pears; place them, one at a time, into Chianti mixture. Add enough water to completely cover pears. Simmer until pears are tender but not mushy, 15 to 30 minutes depending on variety. Cool pears in liquid; transfer to bowl.

Pears Poached in Chianti

3 Return pan to medium heat; simmer about 10 to 15 minutes or until liquid is reduced by 2/3. Strain sauce; discard spices. Set 1 pear on each of 6 serving plates; spoon sauce on top. Garnish with mint sprigs; serve immediately. For 12 servings, cut pears in half before serving.

6 to 12 servings.

POLENTA AND HAZELNUT BISCOTTI

These biscotti are sweet and fragrant, with a wonderfully crunchy texture.

Butter and flour for baking sheet
2   cups all-purpose flour, plus more as needed
1   cup medium-ground yellow polenta
3/4 cup granulated sugar
1½ teaspoons baking powder
1/4 teaspoon salt
3   eggs, lightly beaten
1   tablespoon unrefined corn or olive oil
1   teaspoon vanilla
1   cup hazelnuts, toasted, skinned*
1   egg white mixed with 1 tablespoon water

1   Heat oven to 400°F. Lightly butter and flour baking sheet. In large bowl, combine 2 cups flour, polenta, sugar, baking powder and salt; mix briefly. Add eggs, oil, vanilla and hazelnuts; mix, scraping sides as necessary, until mixture comes together as coarse, sticky dough. Transfer dough to floured work surface; gather it into a ball. Divide dough into 4 equal portions.

2   Roll each portion into 10x1-inch rope. Place rolled lengths on baking sheet at least 4 inches apart. Just barely flatten surface of each length; brush tops with the egg white mixture. Bake 20 minutes or until loaves just begin to color.

3   Remove from oven; reduce temperature to 325°F. Cool loaves 5 minutes. Cut into 1-inch-wide diagonal slices; arrange on ungreased baking sheet. Return to oven; bake 5 to 8 minutes or until dry. Transfer to wire rack to cool completely. Store in airtight container.

   TIP *To skin hazelnuts, place nuts on baking sheet. Bake at 350°F 8 to 12 minutes or until lightly toasted. Place on kitchen towel; cover with second towel. Cool slightly. Briskly rub hazelnuts with towel until skins flake off. A few stubborn skin remnants may remain, which is okay.

About 3½ dozen cookies.

DISCOVERING MOROCCO

Kitty Morse

TAGINE OF ROCK CORNISH HENS WITH PRUNES AND ALMONDS | SWEET COUSCOUS TIMBALES | GRILLED PEPPER AND AVOCADO SALAD

From displays of couscous on supermarket shelves to sumptuous tagines gracing the cover of popular food magazines, Morocco's cuisine is finally gaining the recognition it deserves in the United States. Fortunately, the ingredients necessary to cook à la marocaine, *from cilantro to saffron, are readily available today.*

Like most cooks, I find inspiration in the bounty of the season — be it in a lustrous eggplant to make a cumin-scented Zahlouk (the Moroccan version of ratatouille), or in the sweet red bell peppers and velvety ripe avocados needed to assemble a colorful palette that reminds me of the Moroccan flag.

Morocco's tagines include myriad seasonal combinations of fish, meat or fowl with vegetables, and often fruit. Each one calls for its own unique combination of herbs and spices. For me, the Tagine of Rock Cornish Hens with Prunes and Almonds, *a classic of the Moroccan repertoire, is a delicious case in point. So is Morocco's staple, couscous, my favorite comfort food. In Morocco, couscous is traditionally topped with a number of seasonal vegetables, lamb, or chicken simmered in a saffron-infused broth. Couscous' versatility and ease of preparation, however, often inspires me to serve it as a substitute for pasta or rice.*

In spite of these modern adaptations, I adhere to tradition when it comes to dessert. To my mind, there is no better way to conclude a Moroccan meal than with a platter of seasonal fruit and a glass of freshly brewed mint tea.

ZAHLOUK   ORANGE SLICES IN ORANGE BLOSSOM WATER   MINT TEA

TAGINE OF ROCK CORNISH HENS WITH PRUNES AND ALMONDS

Morocco is famous for its tagines — mouth-watering combinations of meat, poultry or seafood, and seasonal vegetables, or sometimes, fresh or dried fruit. The essence of each tagine lies in the judicious pairing of exotic spices and fresh herbs used to flavor the sauce. The word tagine also refers to the earthenware cooking implement with its conical lid. Tagines are usually served on their own with plenty of crusty bread to mop up the sauce. This tagine of prunes, honey and cinnamon is a Moroccan classic. Use a pan that can go from stovetop to oven, such as a medium, heavy, enameled Dutch oven or baking dish for best results.

2 tablespoons olive oil	5	large onions, thinly sliced
1 teaspoon ground turmeric	1/2	teaspoon ground cinnamon
1 teaspoon ground ginger	1/2	cup chicken broth
1 teaspoon salt	2	tablespoons honey
1/2 teaspoon freshly ground pepper	6	oz. pitted prunes, plumped in warm water, drained
8 threads Spanish saffron, toasted, crushed*	2	tablespoons butter
2 garlic cloves, minced	1/2	cup whole blanched almonds
6 small or 3 large Cornish hens, washed, patted dry		

1 In large bowl, combine oil, turmeric, ginger, salt, pepper, saffron and garlic; mix well. Coat hens inside and out with mixture; set aside. Line bottom of medium Dutch oven or enameled pan with onion slices. Sprinkle with cinnamon. Cook, stirring occasionally, over medium-high heat, about 8 to 10 minutes or until onions are tender. Set hens snugly on top of onions; add broth and honey. Cover; reduce heat to medium. Cook about 45 to 50 minutes or until hens are tender. Sprinkle prunes around hens.

2 Heat oven to 425°F. Transfer pan to oven; remove lid. Bake about 15 to 20 minutes or until sauce reduces by 1/3 and hens are no longer pink in center.

3 Meanwhile, in small skillet, melt butter over medium-high heat. Fry almonds, shaking pan back and forth, until nuts turn golden brown. Drain on paper towels; set aside.

4 To serve, cut large hens in half or leave small ones whole. Arrange on serving platter. Pour sauce and prunes over hens; sprinkle with almonds. Serve with crusty bread or couscous.

TIP *To toast saffron, place threads in small skillet over medium-high heat; shake gently until threads darken slightly. (Do not overcook or saffron will turn bitter.) Reduce saffron to a powder with a dash of salt; proceed with recipe.

Tagine of Rock Cornish Hens with Prunes and Almonds

6 servings.

SWEET COUSCOUS TIMBALES

A steaming platter of sweet couscous is one of the numerous dishes served during a celebration in Morocco. This colorful timbale *is one of my adaptations, and it makes a delicious accompaniment to a tagine or even roasted fowl.*

2	tablespoons olive oil	8	dried apricot halves, diced
1	medium onion, finely diced	1 1/2	cups couscous
1 3/4	cups chicken broth	1/4	cup frozen baby peas, thawed
1	teaspoon sweet Hungarian paprika (optional)	1	tablespoon orange blossom water** (optional)
1/8	teaspoon salt	1/3	cup golden raisins plumped in warm water, drained
1/8	teaspoon freshly ground pepper		
4	threads Spanish saffron, toasted, crushed*	2	tablespoons fried almonds*** (optional)

1 In medium saucepan, heat oil over medium-high heat until hot. Add onion; sauté until tender. Add broth, paprika, salt, pepper, saffron and apricots. Bring to a boil. Gradually stir in couscous and peas; remove from heat. Cover; let stand 12 to 15 minutes. Transfer couscous to bowl; add orange blossom water.

2 Lightly oil small (6-oz.) ramekin or bowl; pack with 2/3 cup couscous mixture. Cover with warmed dinner plate; invert to unmold. Repeat with 5 remaining dinner plates. Garnish with raisins and fried almonds. (*Couscous can be reheated in microwave if needed.*)

TIPS *To toast saffron, place threads in small skillet over medium-high heat; shake gently until threads darken slightly. (Do not overcook or saffron will turn bitter.) Reduce saffron to a powder with a dash of salt; proceed with recipe.

**Orange blossom or orange flower water is available in Middle Eastern markets, specialty markets or large liquor stores.

***See Tagine of Cornish Game Hens recipe (page 60, step 3) to see how to fry almonds.

6 servings.

GRILLED PEPPER AND AVOCADO SALAD

A Moroccan meal usually begins with an assortment of cooked or raw salads. Here is an adaptation of the classic cumin-scented grilled pepper salad which is here, spooned over slices of ripe avocado.

3	large red bell peppers	1/8	teaspoon freshly ground pepper
3	ripe avocados	2	tablespoons extra-virgin olive oil
	Juice of 1/2 lemon (about 2 tablespoons) or to taste	1	teaspoon ground cumin
1/8	teaspoon salt	2	green onions (white parts only), sliced

1 Heat broiler. Grill bell peppers, turning carefully with tongs until skins blister evenly. Place grilled peppers in bowl or plastic bag; cover. When cool, peel and seed peppers; dice finely. Place in colander to drain.

2 Peel and seed avocados; cut into thin slices. Arrange artfully on serving platter or individual salad plates. Sprinkle avocado with a little lemon juice to prevent discoloration.

3 In bowl, combine grilled peppers with remaining lemon juice, salt, pepper, oil and cumin; mix well. Spoon over avocado slices. Sprinkle with green onions; serve immediately.

6 servings.

Grilled Pepper and Avocado Salad

ZAHLOUK

MOROCCAN EGGPLANT SALAD

Think of Zahlouk as a cumin-scented ratatouille. During eggplant season, Zahlouk appears daily on most Moroccan tables. There are as many versions of Zahlouk as there are cooks. I like to prepare this chunky version, and then blend any leftovers to make a delicious dip. Like most Moroccan salads, Zahlouk tastes best when served at room temperature.

Zahlouk

1	large globe eggplant
2	tablespoons olive oil
3	tomatoes, peeled, seeded, coarsely chopped
2	garlic cloves, minced
2	tablespoons tomato paste
1	teaspoon sugar
1	bay leaf
2	teaspoons ground cumin
	Salt and freshly ground pepper to taste
1 to 2	teaspoons fresh lemon juice
	Fresh cilantro sprigs

1   Heat oven to 350°F. Pierce eggplant with fork in several places; place in baking pan. Bake until soft, about 1 hour depending on size. Cut eggplant in half; cool. When cooled, scoop out flesh; chop coarsely. Set aside.

2`   In large skillet, heat oil over medium-high heat until hot. Stir in tomatoes, garlic, tomato paste, sugar and bay leaf. Cook about 10 minutes or until most of the tomato liquid evaporates.

3   Stir in eggplant pulp, cumin, salt and pepper. Reduce heat to low. Continue cooking about 10 to 15 minutes or until most of the liquid evaporates. Discard bay leaf. Transfer to serving dish; stir in lemon juice. Garnish with cilantro. Serve at room temperature.

6 servings.

ORANGE SLICES IN ORANGE BLOSSOM WATER

This quintessential Moroccan dessert is as refreshing and fragrant as it is easy to prepare.

8   Valencia oranges
2   tablespoons orange blossom water*
    Ground cinnamon
8   fresh spearmint leaves, finely chopped

1   Peel oranges, removing all rind, white pith and seeds. Cut into 1/4-inch thick slices; arrange on serving plate. Sprinkle with orange blossom water, cinnamon and mint. Serve chilled.

> TIP *Orange blossom or orange flower water is available in Middle Eastern markets, specialty markets or large liquor stores.

6 servings.

MINT TEA

Mint Tea *is the national drink of Morocco. The syrupy sweet beverage is served in special mint tea glasses, usually along with dessert.* Mentha veridis, *or spearmint, is the preferred mint for tea. Moroccans use Chinese Gunpowder green tea, which is available in the U.S. in specialty markets. Do not substitute black tea or Japanese green tea.*

5   cups boiling water
2   teaspoons Chinese Gunpowder green tea
1/2   cup sugar or to taste
1   large bunch (at least 20 branches) fresh spearmint, rinsed under running water

1   Swirl a little boiling water in teapot to warm; discard water. Add tea; cover with remaining boiling water. Let steep 2 to 3 minutes. Add sugar and mint. Let stand 3 to 4 minutes. Serve immediately in small tea cups or mint tea glasses. Can also serve chilled over ice.

6 servings.

Orange Slices in Orange Blossom Water

FRENCH DESSERT BUFFET

Mary Evans

| QUATRE-QUARTS MARBRE | CHOCOLATE COEUR A LA CREME | ROULADE A L'ORANGE |

The French make wonderful pastries. My satisfied smile of contentment at the end of each meal while in France is proof positive that good ingredients and a love of cooking can make the most wonderful things happen.

I love to bake, so much so that I went to a professional baking school called Lenôtre in the outskirts of Paris to perfect my skills. When I get home from leading food tours in Paris, I like to re-create some the scrumptious treats I've sampled. So I often pull out my notes from classes to help make them as closely as possible. One of my favorite ways to share these results is to invite friends in for a dessert buffet. Everyone tries a little of everything and has a great time: You can tell by the satisfied smile of contentment they wear afterwards!

So here is a nice mix of dessert textures and flavors that can easily be served buffet style. There's a pound cake, a creamy heart-shaped dessert for the choco-holic, an orange rolled cake and two bite-sized tempters for plate-less grazing.

HAZELNUT PALMIERS | FRANGIPANE TARTELETTES

QUATRE-QUARTS MARBRE

Quatre-quarts *is the French name for pound cake, traditionally made with a quarter pound each of butter, flour, eggs and sugar. Slice this cake into thin or thick pieces depending on whether it's being served as part of a buffet or as an individual dessert.*

       3   tablespoons milk
       2   tablespoons dark rum*
       2   tablespoons Dutch-process cocoa
    1 1/2   cups all-purpose flour
      3/4   teaspoon baking powder
      1/4   teaspoon salt
      3/4   cup unsalted butter, softened
       1   cup sugar
       3   eggs
       2   teaspoons vanilla

1   Heat oven to 350°F. Grease and flour 4 1/2x8-inch bread pan. In small bowl, combine milk and rum. In separate small bowl, stir together cocoa and 2 tablespoons of the milk-rum mixture. In another bowl, sift together flour, baking powder and salt; set aside.

2   In large bowl, beat butter and sugar at medium speed 3 to 4 minutes until very creamy. Beat in eggs, one at a time, just until combined, scraping down sides of bowl frequently. Add 1/2 of flour mixture; beat at low speed just until combined. Beat in remaining milk-rum mixture and vanilla just until combined; beat in remaining flour mixture. Remove 2/3 of batter to medium bowl; beat cocoa mixture into remaining batter. Alternating batters, drop by spoonfuls into pan; swirl with knife.

3   Bake 55 to 60 minutes or until toothpick inserted in center comes out clean and center is firm when pressed with tip of finger. Cool in pan 10 minutes. Remove from pan; cool on wire rack. Slice just before serving.

     TIP *If desired, omit rum and increase milk by 2 tablespoons.

Makes 1 loaf.

Quatre-Quarts Marbré

CHOCOLATE COEUR A LA CREME

Coeur à la crème molds are made of white porcelain and have small holes in the bottom to allow extra moisture from the cream to escape. They can be purchased from specialty cookware shops, or online.

1/3	cup powdered sugar
3	tablespoons unsweetened cocoa
1 1/2	cups heavy whipping cream
1	(8-oz.) pkg. cream cheese, softened
	Cheesecloth
1	quart strawberries

1   In medium bowl, sift together powdered sugar and cocoa; slowly whisk in whipping cream.

2   In large mixer bowl, beat cream cheese at medium speed until softened. Reduce speed to low; slowly beat in whipping cream mixture. Increase speed to medium-high; beat until fluffy. Set aside.

3   Drape several layers of moistened cheesecloth inside coeur à la crème mold.* Spoon whipped mixture into mold. Place mold in shallow pan; cover with plastic wrap. Refrigerate several hours or overnight. When ready to serve, invert onto platter; remove cheesecloth. Serve surrounded with strawberries for dipping. Store in refrigerator.

TIP   *You can use a fine mesh wire strainer over a bowl instead of coeur à la crème mold.

About 3 1/2 cups.

ROULADE A L'ORANGE

Roulade is the French word for roll. This delicate cake stands on its own or, when being served as the only dessert, is great paired with a strawberry puree.

CREME

1/4	cup unsalted butter
	Grated peel of 1 orange
2	tablespoons orange juice
2	tablespoons lemon juice
1/2	cup sugar
1	teaspoon cornstarch
2	eggs

ROULADE

4	eggs, separated
1/2	cup sugar
1 1/2	cups cake flour

1   In small saucepan, heat butter, orange peel, orange juice and lemon juice over medium heat until butter is melted and mixture is bubbling.

2   Meanwhile, whisk together 1/2 cup sugar and cornstarch in small bowl. Whisk 2 eggs together in medium bowl. Slowly whisk in butter mixture; return to saucepan. Stir in sugar-cornstarch mixture; cook over medium-low heat, stirring constantly, until thickened. Do not boil. Immediately pour into clean bowl. Cover surface with plastic wrap; refrigerate several hours until chilled.

3   Heat oven to 400°F. Grease 15x10-inch jelly-roll pan; line bottom with parchment paper. Grease and flour parchment. In large bowl, beat 4 egg yolks at low speed; slowly add 6 tablespoons of the sugar. Increase speed to medium-high; beat about 3 to 4 minutes or until pale yellow and very thick. In clean medium bowl, beat 4 egg whites at medium-high speed about 2 to 3 minutes or until soft peaks form. Add remaining 2 tablespoons sugar and continue beating 1 minute or until stiff but not dry. Fold 1/4 of egg whites into egg yolks. Sift 1/2 of flour over yolk mixture; fold in. Fold in 1/2 of remaining whites, then remaining flour. Fold in remaining whites. Spread mixture into pan.

4   Place in oven; reduce temperature to 375°F. Bake 12 to 14 minutes or until cake is just set. Let cool on wire rack 10 minutes. Cover with parchment paper; invert and unmold. Cool on counter 15 to 20 minutes.

5   To assemble, trim outer edges; spread chilled crème à l'orange over surface of cake. Roll up width-wise, jelly-roll fashion. Slice and serve. For many small servings in a buffet, cake may be rolled lengthwise to form a slender, longer roll.

8 to 10 servings.

Roulade à L'orange

HAZELNUT PALMIERS

Arrange these Hazelnut Palmiers *in a decorative basket for a delightful alternative to cookies.*
Freeze any leftovers, then bring to room temperature as needed for a great accompaniment to
coffee or tea.

1/3 cup sugar
1/4 cup hazelnuts, toasted, skinned*
1 teaspoon water
1/8 teaspoon almond extract
1 egg
1 (17.3-oz.) pkg. frozen puff
    pastry, thawed at room
    temperature 45 minutes

Hazelnut Palmiers

1   Heat oven to 400°F. In food
    processor, combine sugar and
    hazelnuts; process until hazelnuts
    are very finely ground. In small
    bowl, beat water, almond extract
    and egg to form egg wash; set
    aside.

2   On counter, unroll 1 sheet puff
    pastry. Sprinkle with 1/4 of
    hazelnut mixture; rub into surface.
    Turn and repeat. Roll pastry to
    form 10x12-inch rectangle; turn
    so 12-inch side is parallel to
    counter. Fold in 2 shorter sides
    about 2 inches toward center.
    Brush uncovered center 4 inches
    with egg wash; fold each side
    again to cover and meet in center.
    Roll lightly with pin. Brush one
    side with egg wash; fold other side
    over. Roll gently to about 12
    inches in length. Cut in 1/2-inch-
    thick slices; place on baking sheet
lined with parchment. Bake 10 minutes; reduce oven temperature to 350°F. Turn; bake an additional 6
to 8 minutes or until browned and crisp.

3   Meanwhile, prepare other sheet puff pastry as directed above; refrigerate until ready to bake. Return
    oven to 400°F; proceed as directed.

    TIP *To skin hazelnuts, place nuts on baking sheet. Bake at 350°F 8 to 12 minutes or until lightly toasted.
    Place on kitchen towel; cover with second towel. Cool slightly. Briskly rub hazelnuts with towel until skins
    flake off. Some stubborn skins may remain, which is okay.

48 palmiers.

FRANGIPANE TARTELETTES

Frangipane is the French name for almond flavored pastry cream. Dress up these little tarts further with a pitted fresh cherry half when in season.

CRUST
1	cup all-purpose flour
2	tablespoons sugar
1/4	teaspoon salt
1/4	cup unsalted butter, chilled
1	egg yolk
2	tablespoons milk

FILLING
3/4	cup slivered almonds
1/2	cup powdered sugar
1/4	cup unsalted butter, softened
1	egg
3/4	teaspoon almond extract
1/8	teaspoon salt

1   Heat oven to 375°F. In medium bowl, combine flour, sugar and 1/4 teaspoon salt. Cut chilled butter into 1/2-inch cubes; toss with flour mixture. Work butter into flour with fingertips until mixture resembles coarse crumbs. In small bowl, whisk together egg yolk and milk; toss with flour mixture. Work together with fingertips; press into ball. Divide into 16 pieces; roll into walnut-sized balls. Press into mini-muffin pans to cover bottom and sides. Bake 12 to 14 minutes or until set.

2   Meanwhile, in food processor, combine slivered almonds and powdered sugar. Process until nuts are finely ground. Add softened butter, egg, almond extract and 1/8 teaspoon salt; pulse to form paste.

3   When crust is set, divide almond mixture evenly among cups. Bake 15 to 20 minutes or until puffed, browned and set. Serve warm or at room temperature.

16 tartelettes.

SPANISH TAPAS MENU

Michele Anna Jordan

SPANISH TOAST | SAUTEED MUSHROOMS WITH GARLIC AND HAM | CHORIZO SAUTEED IN WHITE WINE AND GARLIC | GARLICKY SHRIMP

he term tapas, I have been told countless times, originated in Spanish bars. To protect a beverage from flies, the story goes, a bartender put a small plate on top of a customer's drink. The story does not say who set the first salted almonds or thin slices of serrano ham (jamón serrano) on one of those plates, but the idea caught on and became a tradition known as tapas. Today, it is popular not only throughout much of Spain but also in the United States, where tapas restaurants are increasingly common. Tapas are presented in small dishes and shared by everyone at the table. Everything except dessert is brought to the table at the same time, as guests enjoy both food and conversation.

Champagne — or cava, as sparkling wine is called in Spain — and dry sherry are the most common beverages served with tapas; both go beautifully with the array of flavors and textures of these dishes. If you prefer wine, look for a Rioja, a delicate red wine from northeastern Spain.

SPANISH TOAST

In Spain, restaurants often have most of the ingredients for this popular dish already on the table. After customers place their orders, hot toast arrives and everybody digs in.

8	thick slices sourdough or other country-style bread
4	large garlic cloves, halved lengthwise
4	ripe tomatoes, halved
	Extra-virgin olive oil
1/8	teaspoon kosher (coarse) salt
1/8	teaspoon freshly ground pepper

1 Toast or grill bread until golden brown on both sides. Rub cut side of 1 garlic half over 1 side of slice of toasted bread, pressing firmly as you rub. Repeat, using a fresh piece of garlic for each slice of toast. Rub each slice of toast with tomato half, pressing firmly to push pulp into toast. Discard tomato skins. Place toast on individual plates; drizzle with a little olive oil. Season with salt and pepper. Serve immediately.

4 to 6 servings.

SAUTEED MUSHROOMS WITH GARLIC AND HAM

Serrano ham — jamón serrano in Spanish — is similar to prosciutto, though it is a little drier and a bit gamier. If you happen to have country-style ham from the American South, you can use it here. If you don't have crimini or portobello mushrooms, use small whole white mushrooms.

1/2	oz. dried cèpes
3/4	cup hot water
3	tablespoons butter
1	shallot, minced
8 to 10	garlic cloves, minced
1	lb. crimini or portobello mushrooms, stems removed, thinly sliced
2 or 3	slices serrano ham or prosciutto, cut into thin crosswise strips
1/8	teaspoon kosher (coarse) salt
1/8	teaspoon freshly ground pepper
2	tablespoons minced fresh Italian parsley

Sautéed Mushrooms with Garlic and Ham

1 In small bowl, soak cèpes in hot water; set aside.

2 In medium skillet, heat butter over medium-low heat until melted. Add shallot; sauté about 5 minutes or until tender and fragrant. Add garlic; sauté an additional 2 minutes. Add mushrooms; cook, covered, 7 to 8 minutes or until mushrooms are limp.

3 Strain liquid covering cèpes; pour it into skillet. Cut cèpes into thin strips; stir into skillet. Increase heat to medium; simmer until liquid is nearly completely evaporated. Stir in serrano ham; cook an additional 2 minutes. Season with salt and pepper. Stir in parsley; transfer to warm serving dish. Cover; serve within 15 minutes.

4 to 6 servings.

CHORIZO SAUTEED IN WHITE WINE AND GARLIC

If you don't have Spanish chorizo, do not use the Mexican kind, which is delicious but too crumbly for this dish. Instead, use linguiça *or* kielbasa.

  1   lb. Spanish chorizo sausage, sliced (3/8 inch thick)
6 to 8   garlic cloves, minced
  3/4   cup dry white wine

1   In medium skillet, sauté chorizo over medium-high heat, stirring occasionally, about 7 to 8 minutes or until sausages release their fat and are just beginning to brown. Pour off all but 1 tablespoon of fat. Return to heat; stir in garlic. Sauté about 2 minutes or until garlic begins to soften, taking care not to burn garlic. Add wine. Increase heat; simmer until wine is nearly completely reduced. Transfer to small serving bowl; serve within 15 minutes.

4 to 6 servings.

Chorizo Sautéed in White Wine and Garlic

Garlicky Shrimp

GARLICKY SHRIMP

The secret to making good shrimp is to begin with fresh (rather than frozen) and to cook shrimp very quickly so they will be juicy rather than dry.

1	lb. shelled, deveined uncooked jumbo shrimp, tails on
1/8	teaspoon kosher (coarse) salt, plus more to taste
	Juice of 1 lemon
2	tablespoons butter
1	tablespoon minced fresh garlic
Scant 1/8	teaspoon crushed red pepper
1/3	cup marsala
1/8	teaspoon freshly ground pepper
1	tablespoon minced fresh Italian parsley

1 Place shrimp in low wide bowl; season with salt. Drizzle with lemon juice; toss. Set aside 15 to 20 minutes.

2 Meanwhile, in medium skillet, melt butter over medium-high heat. Add shrimp, garlic and red pepper; sauté 2 minutes. Turn shrimp over; sauté an additional 30 seconds. Increase heat to high until shrimp turn pink. Carefully add marsala; use a match to set it aflame. When flame dies out, season with salt and freshly ground pepper; remove from heat. Transfer shrimp to warm serving plate; sprinkle with parsley. Serve immediately.

4 to 6 servings.

GRILLED ONIONS WITH SMOKY ROMESCO SAUCE

It is impossible to give an exact cooking time for these onions; test by poking them with a fork or toothpick, which should enter the plumpest portion of the onion with little resistance.

1	recipe *Smoky Romesco Sauce* (recipe follows)
20 to 30	small spring onions or green onions*
2	tablespoons olive oil
1/8	teaspoon kosher (coarse) salt
1/8	teaspoon freshly ground pepper

1   Make Smoky Romesco Sauce. Start charcoal fire about 45 minutes before cooking onions.

2   Remove root end from onions, pulling away any blemished outer leaves. Trim onions so that they are all about the same length. Place onions in large bowl; drizzle with oil. Toss onions in oil using your hands to be sure onions are coated. Spread onions in single layer over moderately hot coals; turn them every few minutes until tender and cooked through, 15 to 25 minutes depending on size. OR, spread onions in single layer on baking sheet; bake in 375°F oven until tender, 15 to 35 minutes depending on size of onions.

Grilled Onions with Smoky Romesco Sauce

3   Transfer onions to serving platter; let rest 5 to 10 minutes. Season with salt and pepper. Serve immediately with Smoky Romesco Sauce on the side.

> TIP *Spring onions refer to onions that have not yet formed a large bulb; you can find them at farmers' markets and better grocery stores from early March through mid-June. They are sweet and delicate, and vary in size.

4 to 6 servings.

SMOKY ROMESCO SAUCE

The chipotle chile adds a delicious Mexican flourish to this classic Spanish sauce.

1/2   chipotle chile
1/2   cup boiling water
  2   tablespoons slivered almonds, toasted*
  3   garlic cloves
  1   pasteurized egg yolk
  1   gypsy pepper or red bell pepper, roasted, peeled, seeded, chopped**
  1   small (2-inch) tomato, peeled, seeded
3/4   cup extra-virgin olive oil
1/8   teaspoon kosher (coarse) salt, plus more to taste
1/8   teaspoon freshly ground pepper, plus more to taste
  2   tablespoons red wine vinegar
  1   tablespoon fresh lemon juice

1   In small bowl, cover chipotle with boiling water; let stand at least 30 minutes.

2   Drain and dry chipotle; remove its stem. In food processor, pulse chipotle, almonds, garlic and egg yolk until mixture is reduced to a smooth paste. Add roasted pepper and tomato; pulse several times. Slowly drizzle in 1/2 of the oil, operating processor continuously. Scrape sides of work bowl; season with salt and pepper. With processor running, add remaining oil. When all of the oil has been incorporated, add vinegar and lemon juice; pulse until smooth. Transfer to bowl, adjust seasonings to taste. Cover; refrigerate 1 hour before using. Sauce will keep, properly refrigerated, about 1 week.

> TIPS *To toast almonds, place on baking sheet; bake at 375°F 6 minutes or until deep golden brown.
>
> **To roast peppers, cut off stem end and remove seed core. Cut in half lengthwise; arrange, cut side down, on baking sheet. Brush lightly with a little olive oil. Bake at 400°F 30 to 45 minutes or until skin blisters. (Time will vary depending on variety of pepper.) Cool to room temperature; peel off skin with your fingers.

About 1 3/4 cups.

TORTILLA ESPANOLA

This ubiquitous tapas is found all over Spain, from children's lunch boxes to out-of-the-way bars and roadhouses. It is usually served with a dollop of allioli, Spain's version of the garlicky mayonnaise known in Provence as aïoli.

1	lb. waxy potatoes, peeled, thinly sliced
1	tablespoon olive oil
1	large yellow onion, very thinly sliced
1	teaspoon kosher (coarse) salt, plus more for seasoning
	Freshly ground pepper
3	garlic cloves, peeled, chopped
1	pasteurized egg yolk
2/3	cup extra-virgin olive oil
1 to 2	teaspoons fresh lemon juice
	Dash cayenne pepper
4	large eggs, lightly beaten

1 In saucepan, cover potatoes with water. Cook over medium heat 12 to 15 minutes or until potatoes are tender but not mushy. Drain thoroughly.

2 In medium nonstick skillet, heat 1 tablespoon olive oil over low heat. Add onion; sauté, stirring occasionally, 25 to 30 minutes or until very tender and sweet. Season with salt and pepper; cool to room temperature.

3 Meanwhile, make allioli. Place garlic in a mortar or suribachi; add generous dash of salt. Crush garlic with wooden mortar, grinding until garlic is reduced nearly to a liquid. Add egg yolk; mix thoroughly. Add extra-virgin olive oil, a few drops at a time, until mixture begins to thicken. Switching to a wooden spoon, continue mixing until all of the oil has been incorporated. Add 1 teaspoon lemon juice, a dash of salt and cayenne pepper; mix thoroughly. Adjust seasonings to taste with remaining lemon juice or more salt if needed. Cover; refrigerate until ready to use.

4 In medium bowl, stir together eggs, potatoes and onion. Season with salt and pepper. Set skillet over medium-low heat; when hot, pour in egg mixture. Cook until eggs are almost but not quite set, about 12 minutes. Carefully slide tortilla onto plate, cooked side down. Invert skillet onto tortilla; turn pan and plate over so tortilla falls into pan, uncooked side down.

5 Return pan to heat; cook until eggs are set. Test by pressing down gently. If tortilla is soft in middle, cook a bit longer.

6 Cool tortilla slightly; cut into wedges. Serve immediately or at room temperature with allioli on the side.

4 to 6 servings.

CREMA CATALAN

In Spain, this tender custard is often served in glazed clay ramekins. These attractive little dishes are readily available in the United States, so use them if you have them. Otherwise use ceramic ramekins; in a pinch, small Pyrex bowls work too.

3   cups half-and-half
1/3 cup sugar
4   (1/2x1-inch) strips lemon peel
4   (1/2x1-inch) strips orange peel
1   vanilla bean
1   (2-inch) cinnamon stick
6   extra-large egg yolks
    Dash kosher (coarse) salt

1   In medium saucepan, cook half-and-half, sugar, lemon peel, orange peel, vanilla bean and cinnamon stick over medium heat. Bring to a simmer, stirring constantly, until sugar is dissolved. Remove from heat; steep, covered, 30 minutes. Strain half-and-half through a fine sieve into clean saucepan. Discard peel and cinnamon. Rinse vanilla bean in cool water; dry it for re-use.

2   Heat oven to 325°F. Have 6 custard cups and a roasting pan large enough to hold them ready.

3   In medium bowl, whisk egg yolks until they turn pale yellow. Set half-and-half over medium-low heat; remove from heat when it just begins to simmer. Mix 1 tablespoon hot half-and-half into egg yolks, followed by another and another, mixing well after each addition. Add salt. Slowly mix in remaining hot half-and-half; pour custard mixture into pitcher or large measuring cup.

4   Pour hot custard into custard cups; place filled cups in roasting pan. Place roasting pan in oven.

5   Pour hot water into roasting pan until it comes about halfway up sides of cups. Cover loosely with aluminum foil.

6   Bake 40 minutes or until each custard is almost but not quite set in middle. Place on wire rack; cool to room temperature. Serve immediately or cover with plastic wrap, chill and serve within 2 days. Store in refrigerator.

6 servings.

HEARTY GERMAN FARE

John Schumacher

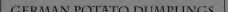

GERMAN POTATO DUMPLINGS | RED CABBAGE | SPAETZLE

No ethnic cookbook would be complete without a chapter on German cuisine. Interestingly enough, the cooking styles of Germany, Austria, Czech Republic, Poland, Netherlands, part of Switzerland, and even France, are similar. In Germany, a schnitzel *is a thinly sliced piece of meat; in France the same item is called a cutlet.*

The German recipes included here are both classic and comforting. Spätzles, German Potato Dumplings *and* Red Cabbage *are often served daily.*

Hasenpfeffer *is a thick German stew of rabbit flavored with peppers, wine and vinegar, served with noodles and dumplings and garnished with sour cream. It is a Sunday or holiday tradition.*

Linzertorte *is a thin tart made with a rich, cookie-like dough containing ground nuts and spices, filled with raspberry/apricot jam and topped with a dough lattice. It is an excellent dessert, but also served for morning and afternoon lunch as well.*

GERMAN POTATO DUMPLINGS

Kartoffelklösse are potato dumplings from the north of Germany. They are made with lean bacon, diced bread and mashed potatoes.

German Potato Dumplings

2 to 3 large russet potatoes (about 1½ lb.)
1 cup all-purpose flour
1 tablespoon grated onion
2 teaspoons salt
½ teaspoon freshly ground pepper
1 egg, separated
48 small garlic croutons*
¼ cup cooked crumbled thick-sliced bacon
¼ cup butter
1½ cups fresh soft bread crumbs
1½ tablespoons chopped fresh parsley

1   Peel and quarter potatoes; boil in salted water until just fork-tender. Drain; let potatoes cool. Put cooled potatoes through ricer. (If using potato masher, use warm potatoes.)

2   In large bowl, thoroughly mix cooled potatoes, flour, onion, salt, pepper and egg. Use ¼ cup mixture for each dumpling. Roll into a ball and press hole in center with thumb. In hole place 3 to 4 croutons and about 1 teaspoon bacon.** Seal tightly by re-rolling ball.

3   In Dutch oven, heat 3 quarts salted water to a fast boil.*** Drop balls into water; return to a boil. Cook 6 to 8 minutes, making sure balls don't stick to the bottom.

4   In skillet, melt butter over medium heat. Stir in bread crumbs and parsley. (*Do not brown.*) Roll cooked dumplings in crumb mixture to coat.****

TIPS *To make garlic croutons, remove crusts from 10 slices of bread of your choice; cut into ½-inch cubes. In large skillet, heat ¼ cup oil. (*I prefer olive oil, but any type of oil will work.*) Sauté 4 garlic cloves until brown; stir in bread cubes. Sauté bread cubes until golden brown. Remove from pan; place on paper towel to absorb oil. Croutons keep at least 1 week.

**For fruit dumplings, place a pitted prune or ½ of a dried apricot inside each dumpling. When dumplings are cooked, remove to a warm plate. Brush with butter; top with powdered sugar.

***I prefer fried dumplings and dumplings stuffed with meat, vegetables, cheese or fruit.

****Uncooked dumplings freeze well. To serve, boil directly from the freezer. Uncooked dumplings stored in refrigerators will turn gray. Leftover dumplings should be fried.

4 servings.

RED CABBAGE

This is one of the classic accompaniments to German and Central European cuisine. It's easy to prepare and can be stored in your refrigerator for up to one week. It is best to make this dish a day or two in advance to let the flavors fuse. Store in a covered container in the refrigerator until needed.

1/4   lb. thick-sliced bacon, diced (1/4 inch)*
1 1/2   cups sliced onions
1 to 2   heads red cabbage, core removed, quartered, sliced (1/4 inch thick)
3/4   cup fresh apple juice
1/2   cup red wine vinegar
1/2   cup red wine
1/2   teaspoon freshly ground pepper
2   garlic cloves, finely minced
1   tablespoon beef base**
2   tablespoons packed brown sugar
1   red apple, cored, diced (1/2 inch)***

1   In large skillet, cook bacon over medium heat until brown and crisp. Add onions; sauté until transparent and tender.

2   Add cabbage, apple juice, vinegar, wine, pepper, garlic, beef base and brown sugar to skillet. Stir well, making sure nothing sticks to bottom of skillet. Reduce heat to low; cover. Cook 20 minutes, stirring gently.**** Add apples; cook an additional 10 minutes.

TIPS *If you are not a fan of bacon, leave it out.

**Beef base is a paste made from reducing beef bones. When purchasing beef base, make sure that the first ingredient is beef — not salt.

***Substitute a red pear for the apple if you wish.

****Be sure not to overcook the red cabbage. It needs to keep some snap to the bite!

8 servings.

SPAETZLE

This dish is one of Germany's supreme contributions to world cuisine. It is not hard to make, but should be approached with respect and care. Spätzle translated from German means "little sparrow." In fact, spätzle are tiny noodles or dumplings made without baking powder. Spätzle keeps about 4 days in the refrigerator.

1/4   cup cold water
2 1/2   teaspoons salt
1/4   teaspoon ground nutmeg
4   eggs
1 3/4   cups all-purpose flour
2   quarts water
      Butter

1   In medium bowl, combine water, 1/2 teaspoon of the salt, nutmeg and eggs; beat with wire whisk until frothy. Slowly add flour until mixture is stiff and gathers around whisk. Remove any mixture from whisk; continue stirring with spoon until mixture comes off sides of bowl.

2   In large saucepan, bring water and remaining 2 teaspoons salt to a boil over medium heat.

3   Put dough into spätzle maker*; drop formed dough into water. Return water to a boil; simmer 1 minute. Remove spätzle from boiling water with slotted spoon; rinse under cold water. Drain well.

4   Line pan with dry, clean kitchen towel. Place spätzle on towel; cover until ready to use.

5   In large skillet, melt butter over medium-high heat. Add spätzle; sauté until hot, taking care not to brown. Spätzle may also be served with pan gravy.**

TIPS *If you don't have a spätzle maker, just press the dough through a deep fat fryer basket.

**You can make a number of variations to this classic side dish by adding chopped parsley, bacon bits, salt, nutmeg, minced onions, shallots and freshly grated Parmesan cheese while sautéing.

4 to 6 servings.

Hasenpfeffer

HASENPFEFFER

Hasenpfeffer *in German means black peppered hare (rabbit). The key is to marinate the rabbit for 3 days in red wine.*

2   rabbits, cut into 6 pieces
3   cups red wine
1   tablespoon fresh lemon juice
1   tablespoon cider vinegar
1/3   cup currant jelly
2   cups sliced onions (1/2 inch thick)
1   cup sliced carrots (1/4 inch thick)
1   cup sliced celery (1/4 inch thick)
2   tablespoons packed brown sugar
2   teaspoons beef base
1   teaspoon salt
1   teaspoon freshly ground pepper
8   juniper berries*
4   bay leaves
4   whole cloves
1   cup seasoned flour**
1/4   cup olive oil
2   teaspoons vegetable oil
8   small gingersnap cookies, crushed

1   Place rabbit pieces in 3-quart casserole. Add wine, lemon juice, vinegar, jelly, onions, carrots, celery, brown sugar, beef base, salt, pepper, juniper berries, bay leaves and cloves. Reserve 1/4 of the marinade. Cover casserole; refrigerate 3 days, turning meat occasionally. Remove rabbit from marinade; discard marinade. Pat rabbit dry. Dredge rabbit in seasoned flour, shaking off excess.

2   Heat oven to 350°F. In Dutch oven, heat olive oil over medium-high heat until hot. Add rabbit; sauté until golden brown on all sides. Pour off any excess oil. Add reserved marinade, onions, carrots and celery; mix well. Place pan in oven. Bake 2 hours or until rabbit is tender. Transfer mixture to clean 3-quart casserole; keep warm. Remove bay leaves from marinade. In blender, blend marinade until smooth.***

3   Pour marinade into pan. Bring to a boil over medium heat; add gingersnaps. Stir well to combine. Pour over rabbit; serve with Spätzle or noodles.

TIPS *If you don't have juniper berries, use 2 oz. gin.

**To make seasoned flour, in a large bowl combine 1 cup all-purpose flour, 2 teaspoons salt and 1/8 teaspoon ground white pepper; mix well.

***If you wish, add 1 1/2 cups sour cream to blended sauce.

4 servings.

LINZERTORTE

First served in the 17th Century, Linzertorte comes from Linzer, Austria. Preparing Linzertorte takes time. You have to assemble ingredients and give yourself a generous amount of time for preparation.

TORTE

- 1 3/4 cups all-purpose flour
- 1 cup finely ground slivered almonds
- 1/2 cup extra-fine granulated sugar
- 1 tablespoon finely shredded lemon peel
- 1/4 teaspoon salt
- 1/8 teaspoon ground cloves
- 1/8 teaspoon ground cinnamon
- 1 cup unsalted butter (no substitutes), chilled, cut into small pieces
- 2 egg yolks, lightly beaten
- 2 teaspoons vanilla
- 3/4 cup apricot preserves
- 3/4 cup raspberry preserves

GLAZE

- 1 egg yolk
- 1 tablespoon whipping cream

TOPPING

- 1/4 cup sifted powdered sugar (optional)

1 In large bowl, sift together flour, almonds, granulated sugar, lemon peel, salt, cloves and cinnamon. Using wooden spoon, beat in butter, 2 egg yolks and vanilla. Place large piece of plastic wrap on baking sheet; place dough on plastic wrap. Pat dough into 10x6-inch rectangle. Wrap in plastic wrap. Refrigerate 1 1/2 hours.

2 In small bowl, combine apricot and raspberry preserves; set aside.

3 Slice off 3/4 of dough crosswise. Cover and chill remaining 1/4 dough. Cut dough crosswise into 3/8-inch strips. Arrange strips around bottom and sides of 10-inch springform pan. Press with fingers to form even crust over bottom and 1 inch up sides of pan. Spread preserve mixture evenly into crust.

4 Place remaining 1/4 dough on floured surface. With floured rolling pin, roll dough into 10x6-inch rectangle. Using floured pastry wheel, cut dough into 10x1/2-inch strips. Carefully lay 6 strips at even intervals across top of filled torte. Give pan 1/4 turn; lay remaining strips on top, forming diamond pattern. Press ends of strips into rim of bottom crust; trim ends as needed. Crimp top edge of crust with tines of fork.

5 In medium bowl, combine 1 egg yolk and whipping cream. Brush pastry strips and edge of torte with egg yolk mixture. Refrigerate 20 minutes. Heat oven to 350°F.

6 Bake 45 to 50 minutes or until lightly browned. Cool on wire rack 1 hour. Loosen springform ring. Cover; refrigerate up to 24 hours. Let stand at room temperature 2 hours before serving. Sprinkle with powdered sugar, if desired.

16 servings.

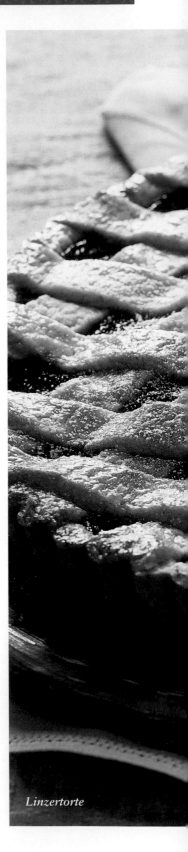

Linzertorte

ENGLISH TRADITIONS

Mary Evans

E very country has its traditional foods, and England is no exception. I've focused on some of them in this menu from the British Isles.

Over recent years, the dining scene in England has improved tremendously. Old favorites, as well as new and innovative dishes, now show care and attention to detail. The country also has a long tradition of excellent cheese making that adds even further depth to its culinary heritage.

A few years ago, I had the opportunity to visit my daughter in London. That visit, and some of the local cookbooks I purchased during the trip, form the basis for the following recipes. We would often stop for quick and casual meals at local restaurants and pubs, sample cheeses or stop for dessert. I've used my memories of delicious Stilton, tasty pub pies and creamy trifles to create this satisfying menu.

SHEPHERD'S PIE | TIPSY TRIFLE

POTTED CHEESE

Potted Cheese is a traditional English method for using up leftover bits of cheese. Use this recipe as a guideline for your own leftover combinations. Use a splash of wine or port plus pinches of seasonings until the flavor is just right.

3/4   cup (3 oz.) crumbled English Cheshire or cheddar cheese
1/2   cup (2 oz.) crumbled Stilton cheese
  3   tablespoons butter, softened
  1   tablespoon port wine
     Dash cayenne pepper
     Dash freshly ground pepper
     Crackers

1   In food processor, pulse cheeses and butter to combine, scraping sides and bottom of bowl frequently. Add port wine, cayenne pepper and pepper; pulse to combine. Serve with crackers.

About 3/4 cup.

Potted Cheese

TOMATO AND WATERCRESS SALAD

Watercress grows wild in streams and ponds throughout England. Its peppery bite complements the sweet-tart taste of tomatoes.

DRESSING

- 2 tablespoons red wine vinegar
- 2 teaspoons Dijon mustard
- 1/4 teaspoon salt
- 1/8 teaspoon freshly ground pepper
- 6 tablespoons canola oil
- 2 tablespoons chopped shallots

SALAD

- 2 heads Bibb lettuce, trimmed, leaves separated
- 3 medium tomatoes
- 2 small or 1 medium bunch watercress, trimmed, leaves separated

Tomato and Watercress Salad

1   In small bowl, whisk together vinegar, mustard, salt and pepper. Slowly whisk in oil; stir in shallots. Set aside.

2   Before serving, line salad plates with lettuce. Halve tomatoes; cut each half into 3 wedges. Fan 3 wedges in circle in center of each plate; place watercress leaves in equal amounts inside tomato circles. Serve with dressing.

6 servings.

SHEPHERD'S PIE

Shepherd's Pie *is an English pub classic. Feel free to substitute equal amounts of beef or venison for lamb if desired.*

2¹/₂ lb. Yukon gold potatoes, peeled, quartered	1 tablespoon fresh minced garlic
2¹/₂ teaspoons salt	1¹/₂ lb. coarsely ground lamb
¹/₄ cup hot milk	1¹/₄ cups reduced-sodium beef broth
2 tablespoons butter	¹/₂ cup red wine
¹/₄ cup fresh minced chives	2 tablespoons tomato paste
2 tablespoons canola oil	¹/₄ teaspoon freshly ground pepper
3 medium carrots, diced	2 tablespoons cornstarch
1 large onion, chopped	2 tablespoons freshly grated Parmesan cheese

1   In large saucepan, cover potatoes with water. Add 1 teaspoon of the salt; bring to a boil over medium-high heat. Reduce heat to medium-low. Simmer 30 minutes or until fork-tender; drain. Return to pan; stir gently over low heat for several minutes to remove excess moisture. Mash with potato masher; continue to mash while adding hot milk and butter until smooth. Add chives and remaining 1¹/₂ teaspoons of salt.

2   Meanwhile, heat oven to 400°F. In large skillet, heat oil over medium-high heat until hot. Add carrots and onion; cook, stirring occasionally, 5 to 8 minutes or until tender and just brown. Stir in garlic; cook 30 to 60 seconds or until fragrant. Add lamb; cook 4 to 5 minutes or until browned. Stir in 1 cup of the beef broth, wine, tomato paste and pepper. Bring to a simmer; reduce heat to low. Simmer 10 minutes.

3   In small bowl, stir cornstarch into remaining ¹/₄ cup beef broth; stir into lamb mixture. Continue simmering; cook 1 to 2 minutes or until thickened. Put lamb mixture in shallow, round 10- to 11-inch baking dish. Spoon mashed potatoes over lamb; sprinkle with Parmesan. Bake 30 minutes or until bubbly and just brown.

6 servings.

TIPSY TRIFLE

Instead of the more customary sherry, this Tipsy Trifle *is laced with a bit of Irish whiskey for a touch of something different. Apricots accentuate the preserves.*

2   cups half-and-half
6   egg yolks
1/2   cup sugar
1   tablespoon cornstarch
3   tablespoons Irish whiskey*
1   (15-oz.) can apricot halves in juice
1/2   cup apricot preserves
2   (3-oz.) pkg. ladyfingers
2   tablespoons chopped fresh mint
1   cup whipping cream
2   tablespoons powdered sugar
     Fresh mint leaves

1   In medium saucepan, simmer half-and-half over medium heat. Meanwhile, in medium bowl, whisk egg yolks and sugar together until combined; whisk in cornstarch. Slowly whisk in hot half-and-half. Return to saucepan; cook, stirring constantly, over medium-low heat until thickened and temperature reaches 160°F. Do not boil. Remove from heat; pour into clean bowl. Stir in 2 tablespoons of the Irish whiskey. Cover; refrigerate 30 minutes or until tepid.

2   Meanwhile, in food processor, puree apricot halves, apricot preserves and remaining tablespoon Irish whiskey. Layer 1 package ladyfingers in bottom of 2-quart clear glass bowl; drizzle with 1/2 of apricot puree. Sprinkle with 1 tablespoon of the chopped mint. Top with 1/2 of whiskey custard. Repeat. Refrigerate overnight to set custard.

3   Before serving, whip cream with powdered sugar until soft peaks form. Top trifle with whipped cream. Garnish with mint leaves. Store in refrigerator.

TIP *While the flavor will change, the Irish whiskey can be omitted if desired. For custard portion, substitute 1 teaspoon grated orange peel for 2 tablespoons whiskey. For apricot mixture, substitute 1 tablespoon lemon juice for 1 tablespoon whiskey.

8 servings.

Tipsy Trifle

CASUAL ASIAN
BUFFET

Jean Yueh

Buffet entertaining is less formal than sit-down meals. Guests enjoy trying a little bit of everything and helping themselves to more of what they like best. Buffets also solve the dilemma of not having ample seating space.

The following recipes, selected from different Asian countries, showcase a variety of contrasting colors and flavors. These recipes are easily multiplied for a larger crowd. Except for grilling the beef for the Indonesian Beef Satay with Peanut Sauce, *this menu can be made ahead.*

CABBAGE SALAD | MARINATED SLICED TOMATOES AND ONIONS | CHINESE NOODLES WITH STIR-FRIED VEGETABLES AND SESAME SEEDS

ROLLED SUSHI WITH SMOKED SALMON AND AVOCADO

Rolled sushi can be made in different sizes. Thin rolls are made with half a sheet of nori and one core ingredient. When several core ingredients are used, use either three-fourths or a whole sheet of nori to contain all the ingredients and form a thicker roll.

RICE

3	cups medium-grain rice (Japanese brand)
3½	cups water
½	cup Japanese rice vinegar
3	tablespoons sugar
1	teaspoon salt

PASTE

¼	cup wasabi powder

FILLING

1	small seedless cucumber
1	ripe firm avocado
4	oz. smoked salmon, thinly sliced
3	cups water
5	tablespoons Japanese rice vinegar
6	(8x7¼-inch) sheets roasted seaweed (sushi nori)
	Japanese soy sauce for dipping
1	(5-oz.) jar Japanese pickled sliced ginger
1	bamboo sushi mat

1 Wash rice 3 or 4 times until water is fairly clear. Drain rice in strainer; let stand 30 minutes. Place rice and 3½ cups water in 3-quart saucepan with well-fitted lid. Bring water to a vigorous boil; reduce heat to very low. Cover saucepan; simmer rice about 20 minutes. Remove saucepan from heat; cover. Let stand 10 minutes.

2 Meanwhile, in small saucepan, heat ½ cup vinegar, sugar and salt until sugar is just dissolved; set aside to cool. Spread hot rice in large bowl. Drizzle vinegar mixture over rice, tossing to distribute seasoning. Do not over-handle rice; let cool before using.

3 Mix ¼ cup wasabi powder with 2 tablespoons plus 2 teaspoons of water or enough water to make a paste. Cover with plastic wrap; let stand at least 10 minutes.

4 Cut cucumber into 7¼-inch lengths; cut each length into ¼-inch thick strips. Peel avocado; cut into ¼-inch thick strips. Divide salmon into 6 thin slices, about 2½x7 inches each. Roll each slice into a thin roll, about 7 inches long.

5 Make a vinegar solution by stirring together 3 cups water and 5 tablespoons vinegar. Use to wet your hands in the next step.

6 For 1½-inch diameter sushi, cut each nori sheet into 1 (6x7¼-inch) sheet. Place bamboo sushi mat on flat surface with short edge nearest you. Place 1 sheet of nori, smooth side down, on mat with wider (7¼-inch) side close to edge of mat nearest you. Place 1 cup rice on nori. Dip hands in vinegar water to prevent sticking as you spread rice evenly to cover nori with your fingertips. Pat rice into an even layer all the way to sides of nori, leaving ¾-inch border at bottom end of wider side of nori.

7 Using finger, spread a pinch of wasabi paste across center of rice. Place 1 cucumber strip across center of rice from end to end. Top with a few avocado strips and 1 salmon roll. Hold ingredients firmly in place with your fingertips; with your thumbs, fold nori around filling and rice, leaving uncovered border of nori for end of roll. Roll into firm log. Gently but firmly press bamboo mat around roll about 30 seconds to smooth out roll. Repeat with remaining ingredients to make 5 more rolls. They can be made a few hours ahead, but do not refrigerate as rice will get hard.

8 Just before serving, dip sharp knife in cold water; cut each roll crosswise into 6 or 8 even pieces. Clean knife between cuts when needed. Serve sushi rolls, cut side up, on platter accompanied with wasabi paste, soy sauce and pickled ginger.

36 or 48 pieces.

Rolled Sushi with Smoked Salmon and Avacado

INDONESIAN BEEF SATAY WITH PEANUT SAUCE

The meat is well-marinated and seasoned before grilling. Adjust the spiciness by using more or less crushed red pepper. This satay tastes best when cooked over a charcoal grill, but it can also be cooked on a stove-top grill or under a broiler.

10 (6- to 8-inch) bamboo skewers soaked in water at least 1 hour

MARINADE
6 tablespoons vegetable oil
1 cup minced shallots
1/4 cup minced fresh garlic
4 teaspoons minced fresh ginger
1/4 cup sugar or to taste
2 1/2 teaspoons salt or to taste
4 teaspoons ground coriander
1/2 teaspoon crushed red pepper or to taste
1/2 teaspoon freshly ground pepper or to taste
1 stalk lemongrass, minced

BEEF
2 lb. boneless sirloin (about 1-inch thick) cubed 1 inch (or chicken breast or 1 lb. each of beef and chicken)

PEANUT SAUCE
1 1/2 tablespoons vegetable oil
6 garlic cloves, minced
1 to 2 teaspoons crushed red pepper or to taste
1 cup creamy peanut butter
1 cup unsweetened canned coconut milk
1/2 cup reduced-sodium chicken broth or water
3 tablespoons Indonesian sweet soy sauce* or to taste
1 1/2 teaspoons salt or to taste
2 tablespoons plus 2 teaspoons fresh lime juice or to taste

Indonesian Beef Satay with Peanut Sauce

1 In wok or saucepan, heat 6 tablespoons oil over medium heat. Add shallots, 1/4 cup garlic and ginger; sauté 3 minutes, taking care not to burn garlic. Stir in sugar, salt, coriander, 1/2 teaspoon red pepper, black pepper and lemongrass; stir until sugar is dissolved. (*Marinade is more like a paste.*) Let cool to room temperature before mixing with meat. (*If both chicken and beef are used, divide marinade into 2 equal portions; marinate in separate containers.*) Marinate at least 8 hours or preferably overnight.

2 In saucepan, heat 1 1/2 tablespoons oil over medium heat. Add 6 garlic cloves and 1 to 2 teaspoons red pepper; sauté 1 to 2 minutes, taking care not to burn garlic. Add peanut butter, coconut milk, broth and soy sauce. Stir and cook until well mixed. If sauce is too thick, add more coconut milk or broth; if sauce is too thin, add more peanut butter. Stir in salt and lime juice; adjust seasonings to taste.

3 Heat grill or broiler. Place 4 to 5 beef cubes on skewers. Cook on all sides 8 to 10 minutes, turning a few times, until meat is no longer pink in center. Serve with warm Peanut Sauce.

TIP *Indonesian sweet soy sauce is available in Asian markets. If unavailable, replace with 3 tablespoons Japanese soy sauce and 2 tablespoons plus 1 teaspoon brown sugar; reduce salt to 1/2 teaspoon or to taste.

8 servings.

VIETNAMESE CHICKEN AND CABBAGE SALAD

This is a very popular dish in Vietnam. It is sort of a Vietnamese version of coleslaw, but is much lighter. Mint adds a refreshing taste to this salad.

SAUCE
3 tablespoons sugar or to taste
1 teaspoon crushed red pepper or to taste
4 shallots, finely sliced
1 garlic clove, minced
1/4 cup fresh lime juice or to taste
1/4 cup fish sauce* or to taste
3 tablespoons vegetable oil
2 tablespoons white rice vinegar

SALAD
8 cups finely shredded Savoy cabbage
1/2 lb. cooked chicken breast, shredded** (2 cups)
2 carrots, cut into matchstick-size strips (1/8x1/8x2 1/2-inch)
1/2 cup shredded fresh mint or to taste
Fresh mint sprigs

1 In medium bowl, combine sugar, red pepper, shallots, garlic, lime juice, fish sauce, vegetable oil and white rice vinegar; let stand 15 minutes or until sugar is dissolved.

2 In serving bowl, combine cabbage, chicken, carrots and 1/2 cup mint. Toss with sauce; adjust seasonings to taste. Garnish with mint sprigs just before serving.

TIPS *Look for fish sauce, used throughout southeast Asia in much the same way as soy sauce, in the Asian section of supermarkets.

** To cook chicken breast: In 3-quart saucepan, boil 2 quarts water, making sure there is enough water to cover chicken. Add 1 (1-lb.) whole chicken breast, bone-in with skin. Return water to a boil; immediately reduce heat to low. Cover; simmer on very low heat about 25 minutes or until chicken is no longer pink in center. (*For an electric stove, set one burner on high and one on low, so saucepan can be immediately transferred from high to low.*) Immediately remove chicken from saucepan; rinse thoroughly with cold water.

8 to 10 servings.

MARINATED SLICED TOMATOES AND ONIONS

This dish tastes best when using vine-ripened tomatoes. However, the marinade will perk up the flavor of even not-quite-in-season tomatoes.

1   medium onion
2   lb. ripe firm tomatoes (pick similar size), sliced (3/8-inch thick)
2   tablespoons Asian sesame oil
1/4 cup rice vinegar or to taste
4   teaspoons sugar (more for winter tomatoes)
1   teaspoon salt or to taste

1   Cut onion into very thin slices, about 1/16 inch; separate into individual rings. Place tomatoes and onion in large, shallow container. Sprinkle with oil, vinegar, sugar and salt, making sure marinade covers all tomato slices. Let stand 30 minutes or longer, turning vegetables a few times before serving.

8 servings.

CHINESE NOODLES WITH STIR-FRIED VEGETABLES AND SESAME SEEDS

This dish can be made ahead and served at room temperature. You can also serve it warm. To do this, cook the noodles and drain in a colander, but don't rinse with cold water. Toss warm noodles with sesame oil and soy sauce, then mix with just-cooked vegetables and sesame seeds.

1 lb. fresh Chinese egg noodles or dried vermicelli
2 tablespoons Asian sesame oil
6 tablespoons soy sauce or to taste
2 tablespoons vegetable oil
2 medium carrots, cut into matchstick-size strips ($1/8$x$1/8$x$21/2$-inch)
1 lb. zucchini, cut into matchstick-size strips ($1/4$x$1/4$x3-inch)
8 oz. crimini or button mushrooms, sliced ($1/4$ inch thick)
$1/4$ cup sesame seeds, toasted*

1 In large saucepan, bring 4 quarts water to a boil over medium-high heat. Add fresh noodles; cook 4 minutes or until tender but still a little chewy. (*If dried vermicelli is used, cook according to package directions.*) Quickly drain in colander; rinse with cold water. Drain well. In large bowl, toss noodles with sesame oil and 2 tablespoons of the soy sauce.

2 Heat wok or large skillet over medium-high heat until hot. Add vegetable oil. When oil is hot, add carrots; sauté about 1 minute. Add zucchini and mushrooms; stir-fry 1 minute. Stir in 2 tablespoons of the soy sauce. Cook and stir until zucchini is somewhat soft but still crisp. Add vegetables and sesame seeds to noodles; toss to mix. Add remaining soy sauce to taste.

TIP *To toast sesame seeds, heat small skillet over medium heat. Add sesame seeds; shake skillet continuously until seeds are lightly browned, 3 to 4 minutes.

8 to 10 servings.

Chinese Noodles with Stir-Fried Vegetables and Sesame Seeds

CELEBRATING
PROVENCE

Michele Anna Jordan

BLACK MUSSELS STEAMED IN PASTIS, HERBS AND GARLIC | WARM FRISEE SALAD WITH GOAT CHEESE, GRAPES AND TAPENADE CROUTONS

P rovence, in southern France, stretches westward from Italy and the Côte d'Azur to the Languedoc. Its northern borders embrace the Southern Rhône region, the location of one of the world's greatest wine appellations, Châteauneuf-du-Pape. Provence is bordered on the south by the Mediterranean Sea. The land is shaped by cycles of drought and flood, and its rocky soil is hospitable to grapevines, goats and olive trees.

Signature ingredients shape the cuisine of Provence, revealing these many influences. You'll find fish and shellfish from the sea, olive oil from one of the dozens of mills in the region, goat cheese, and (perhaps surprisingly) polenta, introduced when the region was part of Italy. Wild mushrooms thrive in much of Provence, as does the black truffle. Provence's lavender honey is considered one of the finest honeys in the world.

The food in Provence is, of course, French. But it is rustic and regional, defined by the land and by the seasons rather than by classic techniques and mother sauces, as French haute cuisine is. It is a style perfectly suited to the home cook.

ROAST DUCKLING WITH HONEY AND GARLIC | OVEN POLENTA WITH CARAMELIZED SHALLOTS AND WILD MUSHROOMS | RUSTIC STRAWBERRY TART

BLACK MUSSELS STEAMED IN PASTIS, HERBS AND GARLIC

Pastis and its cousin Pernod are afternoon aperitifs popular throughout Provence. The subtle licorice flavor of pastis resonates beautifully with fresh tarragon. To make this dish without it, use white wine and omit the tarragon sprigs.

2	tablespoons butter
1	shallot, minced
6	garlic cloves, minced
3/4	cup pastis or pernod
2	fresh Italian parsley sprigs
2	fresh tarragon sprigs
2	fresh thyme sprigs
1	fresh oregano sprig
	Grated peel of 1 lemon
3	lb. black mussels, scrubbed, debearded if necessary
12	slices country-style bread, toasted

1 In large saucepan, melt butter over medium heat. Add shallot; sauté 4 to 5 minutes. Add garlic; sauté 1 minute more. Add pastis, parsley, tarragon, thyme, oregano and lemon peel. Carefully add mussels; cover pan. Cook until mussels just open, 3 to 4 minutes. Uncover; simmer until sauce is slightly thickened. Discard herbs and any unopened mussels.

2 Divide mussels among large soup bowls. Spoon some sauce over each portion; serve immediately with bread.

6 servings.

Black Mussels Steamed in Pastis, Herbs and Garlic

WARM FRISEE SALAD WITH GOAT CHEESE, GRAPES AND TAPENADE CROUTONS

Contrasts in flavor and texture — sweet grapes and salty bacon, bitter greens and tangy cheese — are the highlights of this salad, along with the wonderful croutons.

1	large or 2 small heads frisee, trimmed, leaves separated		Kosher (coarse) salt
4	oz. young goat cheese such as chabis		Freshly ground pepper
3	thick slices bacon, diced	1/3	cup extra-virgin olive oil
1	shallot, minced	2	cups red flame grapes, halved
3	tablespoons aged white wine vinegar or sherry vinegar	2/3	cup *Tapenade* (recipe follows)
		12	toasted baguette croutons

1 Tear frisee into medium pieces; put it in wide bowl. Break goat cheese into pieces; scatter over frisee.

2 In medium skillet, fry bacon over medium heat until just barely crisp. Reduce heat to medium-low. Add shallot; sauté 5 minutes or until tender and fragrant. Add vinegar; season with salt and a generous amount of pepper. Add olive oil; heat through. Remove from heat.

3 Pour dressing over greens; toss gently. Add grapes; toss again. Divide among individual plates. Quickly spread tapenade on each crouton; place 2 croutons on each serving. Serve immediately.

6 servings.

TAPENADE

A tapenade can be course and chunky or smooth and velvety, but should include the basic ingredients of olives, anchovies, garlic, capers, and, of course, olive oil.

2	garlic cloves	1	tablespoon minced fresh Italian parsley
1	anchovy fillet		
6	oz. mixed olives, pitted, minced	2	teaspoons minced fresh basil
2	teaspoons capers, drained		Freshly ground pepper

1 Using a mortar and pestle or suribachi, pound garlic and anchovy into a smooth paste. Add olives; using pestle, mix until olives, garlic and anchovy are mostly but not totally smooth. Add capers; crush gently with pestle. Using rubber spatula, fold in parsley and basil. Season with pepper; cover. Set aside until ready to use.

About 2/3 cup.

Warm Frisée Salad with Goat Cheese, Grapes and Tapenade Croutons

ROAST DUCKLING WITH HONEY AND GARLIC

Lavender honey — honey from bees that feed on lavender flowers, not honey scented with lavender — from Provence is famous all over France, and beyond. This honey has a rich, deep flavor and has become widely available in the United States.

1/2 cup kosher (coarse) salt, plus more to taste
2 ducklings, about 4 lb. each
  Freshly ground pepper
1 small onion, halved
10 garlic cloves, unpeeled
2 large garlic cloves, peeled
  Olive oil
1/3 cup honey, preferably lavender honey, warm
1/3 cup red wine vinegar

1   Fill large stockpot 2/3 full with water; add 1/2 cup salt. Bring to a boil over high heat.

2   Remove duck innards from large cavity; reserve for another recipe. Rinse duck inside and out under cool tap water; dry on tea towels. Using tip of a sharp knife, pierce duck skin in several places. Place 1 duck in boiling water. When water returns to a boil, remove duck; place it on rack set over clean tea towels. Repeat with remaining duck. Use a hair dryer to thoroughly dry the ducks' skin.

3   Heat oven to 450°F. Set rack in large roasting pan.

4   Season cavities of both ducks with salt and pepper; place 1/2 onion and 5 garlic cloves inside each. Halve garlic cloves; rub cut sides over duck skin, pressing clove firmly into skin. Using your hands, rub a little olive oil on duck skin. Season all over with salt and pepper. Truss ducks.

5   In medium bowl, combine honey and vinegar; season generously with pepper.

6   Place ducks on their sides on roasting rack; set in oven with breasts facing back of oven. Bake 10 minutes. Turn ducks over; bake an additional 10 minutes. Set ducks upright; reduce temperature to 400°F. Bake 20 minutes. Using pastry brush, coat ducks all over with honey mixture; return to oven. Bake 20 to 25 minutes or until juices run clear (about 15 minutes per pound total cooking time). Baste skin with honey mixture 2 or 3 times as it cooks.

7   Remove from oven; season with salt and pepper. Cover with tent of aluminum foil; let rest 20 to 30 minutes before carving. Carve duck; arrange on platter. Season lightly with salt and pepper; serve immediately.

6 servings.

OVEN POLENTA WITH CARAMELIZED SHALLOTS AND WILD MUSHROOMS

Polenta baked in the oven develops a rich, full corn flavor.

6	cups water
1 1/2	cups coarse-ground polenta
2	teaspoons kosher (coarse) salt, plus more to taste
2	tablespoons unsalted butter
6	shallots, pceled, very thinly sliced
1	teaspoon fresh thyme, minced
	Freshly ground pepper
3/4	cup (3 oz.) grated dry jack cheese
1	lb. chanterelles or other wild mushrooms
1/2	cup dry white wine
	Fresh thyme sprigs

1　Heat oven to 350°F. Pour water into 2-quart Pyrex or soufflé dish; whisk in polenta and 2 teaspoons salt. Bake, uncovered, 40 minutes.

2　In small skillet, melt butter over medium-low heat. Add shallots; sauté 3 to 4 minutes or until tender. Season with salt; reduce heat to very low. Continue cooking, stirring occasionally, 25 to 30 minutes or until shallots are very soft and sweet. (*Do not let them burn.*) Stir in minced thyme; season with pepper. Remove from heat.

3　After 40 minutes, stir polenta with a wooden spoon. Stir in cheese and all but a generous spoonful of shallots. Return to oven 10 to 15 minutes or until liquid is completely absorbed and polenta is tender.

4　Meanwhile, return pan with shallots to medium heat. Add mushrooms and wine; cover. Cook about 10 minutes or until mushrooms are tender. Uncover; simmer until liquid is almost completely reduced. Season with salt and pepper; remove from heat.

5　Spoon mushrooms on top of polenta; garnish with thyme sprigs. Serve immediately.

6 servings.

RUSTIC STRAWBERRY TART

A pie or tart with a free-form crust such as this one is known as a galette. Galettes are made with a variety of sweet and savory fillings. When apricots are in season — in June and early July in most parts of the United States — use them in place of the strawberries.

1¼ cups plus 1 tablespoon all-purpose flour
¼ teaspoon kosher (coarse) salt
3 tablespoons sugar
6 tablespoons unsalted butter, cut into pieces, refrigerated
⅓ cup ice water
4 cups fresh strawberries, stemmed
1 tablespoon butter, melted
1 tablespoon coarse sugar

1   In medium bowl, combine 1¼ cups flour, salt and 1 teaspoon of the sugar. Add butter; use a pastry blender to quickly work butter into flour until it forms a uniform mixture of coarse crumbs. Sprinkle with water; quickly gather dough together, pressing rather than mixing, until it just comes together. Transfer to sheet of plastic wrap; form into ball. Refrigerate 45 minutes.

2   Slice strawberries ¼ inch; place them in medium bowl. Sprinkle with remaining tablespoon flour; toss gently. Add remaining sugar; toss again. Set aside 45 minutes.

3   Heat oven to 400°F.

4   Line baking sheet with parchment paper. Sprinkle work surface with flour; sprinkle flour over a rolling pin. Place chilled dough on work surface; use palm of your hand to flatten it. Roll dough into 14-inch round using rolling pin. Carefully transfer dough to parchment paper.

5   Spread strawberries over dough, leaving 2- to 2½-inch margin of dough. Use your fingers to gently fold edge of dough over strawberries, pleating as you fold. Brush edge with melted butter; sprinkle top with coarse sugar. Bake about 40 minutes or until fruit is soft and bubbly and pastry is golden brown. Cool on wire rack. Serve at room temperature.

6 servings.

Rustic Strawberry Tart

DINNER FROM ITALY

Mary Evans

CAPONATA CROSTINI | SPICY SHRIMP AND LINGUINE | ROASTED PORK WITH FENNEL AND ROSEMARY

America has a love affair with Italian food. We can't get enough, and justifiably so! The cuisine is direct and honest, varying from region to region but united by its universally fabulous results.

The menu here is no exception, starting with crunchy crostini mounded with sweet-tart caponata. Pasta gets all dressed up in the primi course of sporting pasta with a hint of heat. Pop the pork loin into the oven and wait for the wonderful aromas to emerge. Artichokes and potatoes are a traditional pairing and work wonderfully with the roast. Ricotta makes an excellent base for the almondy cheesecake that brings this meal to a delightful close.

ARTICHOKES AND POTATOES AL FORNO   ALMOND-RICOTTA CHEESECAKE

CAPONATA CROSTINI

Caponata hails from the Sicilian portion of Italy. While typically served as a relish, it makes a great topping for the crunchy toast called crostini.

1 medium eggplant, peeled, diced (3/4 inch)	1 tablespoon sugar
3 small tomatoes, diced (1/2 inch)	1 tablespoon tomato paste
1 medium onion, diced (1/2 inch)	1 tablespoon minced fresh garlic
1 red bell pepper, seeded, diced (1/2 inch)	1/2 teaspoon dried oregano, crumbled
3 medium ribs celery, diced (1/2 inch)	1/2 teaspoon salt
2 tablespoons olive oil	1/4 cup red wine vinegar
1/2 cup whole green olives, pitted, coarsely chopped	24 thin slices French bread
2 tablespoons capers, rinsed	

Caponata Crostini

1 Heat oven to 400°F. Place eggplant, tomatoes, onion, bell pepper and celery in shallow 15x10-inch baking pan; toss with oil. Bake 50 minutes, stirring once. Stir in olives, capers, sugar, tomato paste, garlic, oregano, salt and vinegar. Bake 10 minutes. Remove from oven; cool.

2 Meanwhile, reduce temperature to 350°F. Place bread slices on shallow baking sheet; bake 10 to 12 minutes or until crisp and lightly browned. Remove from oven; cool.

3 To serve, mound generous amount of caponata on bread slices.

24 appetizers.

SPICY SHRIMP AND LINGUINE

Green spinach linguine noodles are the perfect foil for pink shrimp and rosy tomato sauce. Banana peppers and crushed red pepper add just the right degree of heat.

1   (12-oz.) pkg. spinach linguine
1   tablespoon olive oil
2   small banana chiles, seeded, diced (about 1/3 cup)
1   (14.5- or 15-oz.) can diced tomatoes in juice
1/2   cup whipping cream
1/8   teaspoon crushed red pepper
1   lb. shelled, deveined uncooked medium shrimp
1/2   teaspoon salt

1 Cook linguine in boiling salted water according to package directions.

2 Meanwhile, in large skillet, heat olive oil over medium heat. Add chiles; sauté 1 to 2 minutes or until slightly softened. Add tomatoes with juice, the whipping cream and crushed red pepper. Cook 5 minutes to reduce and thicken slightly, stirring occasionally. Add shrimp and salt; cook an additional 3 to 4 minutes or until shrimp are cooked through and turn pink.

3 Drain cooked pasta; place in large bowl. Top with shrimp mixture; toss to coat. Divide among 6 pasta bowls.

6 servings.

ROASTED PORK WITH FENNEL AND ROSEMARY

This dish is an adaptation of the classic Italian recipe for porcetta, *a delectable combination of rosemary, fennel and garlic with pork.*

1	tablespoon olive oil
1/2	cup finely chopped fresh fennel
2	garlic cloves
1	teaspoon dried rosemary
1	teaspoon fennel seeds
1/2	teaspoon kosher (coarse) salt
1/8	teaspoon freshly ground pepper
2 1/2	lb. boneless pork loin roast
	Twine
3/4	cup white wine

1 Heat oven to 375°F. In medium skillet, heat oil over medium-low heat until hot. Add fennel; sauté 6 to 8 minutes or until tender.

2 Meanwhile, crush garlic, rosemary, fennel seeds, salt and pepper using mortar and pestle or mini-food processor. Place roast on cutting board, fat side down. Cut down center of roast, lengthwise, to within 1 inch of bottom. Cut each 1/2 segment lengthwise down center of each to within 1 inch of bottom. Cover roast with plastic wrap; tap with rolling pin to flatten slightly. Remove plastic wrap; rub garlic-rosemary mixture over surface. Spread sautéed fennel over all. Roll roast up; tie with twine.

3 Reheat skillet over medium heat until hot. Place roast, fat side down, in skillet; sear fat side only, about 3 to 4 minutes or until lightly browned. Place in shallow roasting pan, fat side up. Add wine to skillet, scraping up any brown bits; pour into roasting pan.

4 Bake 50 to 60 minutes or until internal temperature of roast reads 150°F. Remove from oven; let rest 10 minutes (roast's internal temperature will rise to 155°F). Slice; serve with roasting juices.

6 servings.

*Roasted Pork
with Fennel
and Rosemary*

ARTICHOKES AND POTATOES AL FORNO

Al forno means "in the oven," the perfect way to easily cook a vegetable accompaniment with minimum effort.

2   lb. red potatoes, cut in 1 1/2-inch chunks
2   (9-oz.) pkg. frozen artichoke hearts, thawed
2   tablespoons olive oil
2   tablespoons lemon juice
1/2   teaspoon salt
1/4   teaspoon freshly ground pepper
1/4   cup freshly grated Parmesan cheese

1   Heat oven to 375°F.

2   Place potatoes and artichokes in shallow 15x10-inch baking pan; toss with olive oil and lemon juice.

3   Bake 45 minutes, stirring once, until potatoes are tender. Toss with salt and pepper. Place in serving dish; sprinkle with Parmesan.

6 servings.

ALMOND-RICOTTA CHEESECAKE

Ricotta, an Italian fresh cheese, adds texture to this cheesecake along with almonds in the crust. Almond extract adds a component reminiscent of the Italian liqueur known as amaretto.

1   cup graham-cracker crumbs
1/2   cup slivered almonds
1 1/4   cups sugar
5   tablespoons butter, melted, cooled
2   (8-oz.) pkg. cream cheese, softened
1   (15-oz.) pkg. whole milk ricotta cheese
3   eggs
1   teaspoon almond extract

1   Heat oven to 350°F. In food processor, pulse graham-cracker crumbs, almonds and 1/4 cup of the sugar until almonds are finely ground. Pulse in butter.

2   Press crumb mixture over bottom and 2 inches up sides of 9-inch springform pan. Bake 10 minutes or until crust begins to brown slightly around edges. Remove from oven; cool. Wrap outside of pan bottom and side with aluminum foil.

3   In large mixer bowl, beat cream cheese at medium speed until fluffy. Beat in remaining 1 cup sugar until very soft and creamy; beat in ricotta. Add eggs, one at a time, beating just until combined, scraping down sides frequently. Stir in almond extract. Pour into pan.

4   Bake 60 to 65 minutes or until sides are set but center still moves slightly when gently tapped. Cool on wire rack 1 hour. Refrigerate until chilled; cover. Store in refrigerator.

10 servings.

Artichokes and Potatoes Al Forno

BRUNCH UNDER A MEXICAN SUN

Lisa Golden Schroeder

In Mexico, a typical day opens with coffee and milk (café con leche) and sweet rolls (pan dulce). A later, heartier breakfast (almuerzo) is often eaten to hold appetites until the large afternoon comida Mexicana, *the important family meal of the day. Brunch, the leisurely American-style version of a late breakfast, can be fashioned from this Mexican meal tradition for a weekend gathering of family and friends.*

The markets of Mexico are lush with fresh, ripe, sun-fed tropical fruits. Purees of papaya, mango, watermelon, berries and melons create the base for jewel-toned drinks called Agua Frescas. These refreshing drinks are perfect for kids and grown-ups, almost like drinking a melted fruit popsicle! In contrast, guests who prefer a warm beverage can indulge in spiced Mexican hot chocolate, probably one of the oldest drinks in Mexico.

Then settle everyone down to sausage and egg pockets, or empanadas, served with a fresh salsa rich with avocado. Crispy Fried Plantains and a simple sundae of mango sorbet, fruit and gooey caramel sauce complete this satisfying midday meal.

CRISPY FRIED PLANTAINS | MANGO SORBET AND TROPICAL SALSA WITH CAJETA

AGUA FRESCAS

Agua fresca translates as fresh water *in Spanish. These refreshing fruit drinks (made from fruit, water, lime juice and sugar) go way beyond your usual breakfast orange juice. The popularity of tropical juice blends underscores the appeal of thirst-quenching fruit. Here are two combinations you won't find in the grocery store. For a special touch, freeze small sprigs of fresh mint inside ice cubes to drop into each drink.*

Agua Frescas

CANTALOUPE-MANGO AGUA FRESCA

2 cups seeded coarsely chopped cantaloupe
1 large ripe mango, peeled, sliced
2 to 3 tablespoons sugar
2 to 3 tablespoons lime juice
2 cups cold water
Ice

WATERMELON-STRAWBERRY AGUA FRESCA

2 cups seeded coarsely chopped watermelon
1 cup hulled strawberries, quartered
3 to 4 tablespoons sugar
2 tablespoons lime juice
2 cups cold water
Ice

1 In blender, blend fruit and 1/2 cup water until very smooth. Season to taste with sugar and lime juice. Mix fruit and remaining water in large pitcher, stirring well. Serve over ice.

6 to 8 servings.

MEXICAN SPICED CHOCOLATE

Chocolate is Mexico's gift to the world! The cocoa tree is native to Mexico, and it was the Spanish explorers to the New World who first tasted chocolate in a cool, frothy drink, aromatic with spices and vanilla. The Aztecs of Mexico drank their chocolate unsweetened, but over time sugar was added to it. Today, Mexican chocolate tablets are found in wonderful brightly colored octagonal boxes. The chocolate is sweetened and flavored with cinnamon, vanilla and sometimes almond.

8 cups milk
6 tablespoons almond coffee syrup
4 cinnamon sticks
1 teaspoon whole cloves
2 (3-oz.) tablets Mexican chocolate, chopped
Additional cinnamon sticks, if desired

1 In 4-quart saucepan or small Dutch oven, bring milk, syrup, 4 cinnamon sticks and cloves to a simmer; do not boil. Stir in chocolate; simmer an additional 5 minutes, stirring frequently, until chocolate is melted. Remove cinnamon sticks and cloves with a slotted spoon.

2 Carefully pour chocolate mixture into blender* in small batches; blend until very foamy. Pour into mugs. Repeat with remaining hot chocolate. Serve with cinnamon stick stirrers.

TIP *An immersion or stick blender can be used to froth hot chocolate in a saucepan.

8 servings.

CHORIZO AND EGG EMPANADAS WITH AVOCADO SALSA

Empanadas are pastry turnovers, stuffed with savory or sweet fillings. Large empanadas filled *with a sweet-savory meat and raisin combination called* picadillo *are very traditional, but here a chorizo sausage and egg mixture fits the bill for a morning brunch. Small empanada* (empanaditas) — *bursting with sweet dried fruit pastes — can be found in Mexico for dessert.*

DOUGH
- 2 cups all-purpose flour
- 1 cup yellow cornmeal
- 1 tablespoon baking powder
- 1/2 teaspoon salt
- 1/4 cup cold butter or margarine
- 3/4 cup milk
- 1 egg

FILLING
- 1/2 lb. mild or hot chorizo sausage
- 6 eggs, lightly beaten
- 1/2 teaspoon dried marjoram
- 1 cup shredded *asadero* or Monterey Jack cheese

SALSA
- 8 plum tomatoes, diced (1/4 inch)
- 2 ripe avocado, diced (1/4 inch)
- 1/3 cup finely chopped red onions
- 1/3 cup chopped fresh cilantro
- 2 serrano chiles, stemmed, finely chopped
- 2 garlic cloves, finely chopped

1 To make empanada dough, in large bowl, combine flour, cornmeal, baking powder and salt. Using pastry blender or two knives, cut in butter until mixture resembles coarse meal. Lightly beat together milk and egg; add to flour mixture. Mix with fork until dough forms. Add another tablespoon milk if needed. Gather dough into a ball; knead several times until smooth and pliable. Wrap in plastic wrap; refrigerate up to 1 hour.

2 To make filling, remove sausage from casings; crumble into large nonstick skillet. Cook and stir over medium-high heat until browned. Remove sausage from skillet; drain well on paper towels. Drain fat from skillet; pour in eggs. Cook over medium heat until set. Stir in cooked sausage.

3 Heat oven to 400°F. On floured surface, roll out pastry 1/8 inch thick. Cut out 5-inch rounds. Spoon about 1 1/2 to 2 tablespoons egg mixture onto one side of each pastry round. Sprinkle with cheese. Moisten edges of pastry with water; fold over. Press with fork to seal.

Chorizo and Egg Empanadas with Avacado Salsa

4 Place empanadas on large baking sheets. Bake 15 to 20 minutes or until golden brown.

5 Meanwhile, in large bowl, stir together tomatoes, avocado, onions, cilantro, chiles and garlic. Serve with hot empanadas.

12 to 14 empanadas.

CRISPY FRIED PLANTAINS

Plantains *are a member of the banana family, but are considered "cooking" bananas. They are a staple food in many parts of the world, and are popular fried in Mexico and the Spanish-speaking Caribbean. Longer and thicker than typical eating bananas, plantains must ripen to a nearly black skin color before they become sweet. When cooked, they taste much like potatoes (as do under-ripe eating bananas).*

3 large plantains (skins should be nearly black) or 4 large, green-tip bananas	3/4 teaspoon coarse (kosher) salt
Vegetable oil	1/2 teaspoon ground cumin
	1/4 teaspoon ground cinnamon

1 Peel and cut plantains into 1/4-inch thick diagonal slices.

2 In deep skillet or Dutch oven, heat 1 inch oil to 375°F. Drop plantain slices, several at a time, into hot oil. Cook, turning as needed, 2 to 3 minutes or until golden brown. Drain on paper towel-lined baking sheet. Keep warm in 150°F oven until ready to serve.

3 Meanwhile, combine salt, cumin and cinnamon. Toss fried plantains with seasoning mixture before serving.

6 to 8 servings.

MANGO SORBET AND TROPICAL SALSA WITH CAJETA

Sweet milk (cajeta or dulce de leche), *is a favorite Mexican confection made from caramelized goat's milk and sugar. This golden, sticky sauce can still be found in Mexico made in traditional hammered copper pots (cazos). Cajeta was originally made as a candy filled with nuts and fruits, but is now more generally available commercially canned, to spread on cookies, serve warm over ice cream or use to fill crêpes. Refrigerate any leftover sauce up to 2 weeks.*

SAUCE
1 (12-oz.) can evaporated goat's milk
1/2 cup whipping cream
1 cup sugar
1/2 cup water
1 tablespoon corn syrup
1 tablespoon rum, if desired

SALSA
1 cup diced strawberries (1/4 inch)
1 cup diced fresh pineapple (1/4 inch)
1 cup diced papaya (1/4 inch)
1 tablespoon snipped fresh mint
1 tablespoon fresh lime juice

2 pints mango sorbet
Toasted shredded coconut, if desired

1   To make sauce, combine goat's milk and cream; set aside. In medium saucepan, combine sugar, water and corn syrup; stir until sugar is dissolved. Bring to a boil; cook over medium heat without stirring (*swirl pan occasionally*) until amber in color. Remove from heat; slowly stir in milk-cream mixture (*this will spatter*). Return to medium heat; cook until mixture is smooth. Stir in rum. (*This may be done ahead and refrigerated.*)

2   To prepare salsa, in medium bowl, combine strawberries, pineapple, papaya, mint and lime juice; mix well.

3   To serve, warm sauce if made ahead. Scoop sorbet into dessert bowls. Spoon salsa on top; drizzle with sauce. Sprinkle with coconut.

8 servings.

Mango Sorbet and Tropical Salsa with Cajeta

SCANDINAVIAN CELEBRATION

Beatrice Ojakangas

DILL BUTTERED NEW FINGERLING POTATOES | SMOKED WHOLE SALMON | WILD MUSHROOM SAUCE

he year in Scandinavia is basically divided into two parts: summer and winter. Midsummer falls on June 24th; midwinter, December 24th.

Midsummer is a colorful celebration energized by long sunlit days and nights. People forget the time and stay up all night eating, singing, dancing and visiting. This menu is inspired by a visit to Finland in the summertime, and by Soile Anderson, a popular Twin Cities chef and caterer.

The intensity of 24 hours of sunshine super-charges gardens to create an "explosion" of fresh vegetables and berries in Scandinavia. Baby new potatoes are ready the end of May, and tiny carrots, peas, green beans and fresh dill all come at once. They team to make a wonderfully fresh-tasting, quick and simple soup. Fresh summer salmon is smoked over a barbecue. The forest yields wild mushrooms for the salmon's sauce.

Fresh strawberries add a mellow yet intense flavor to the dessert — a strawberry pudding that can be made ahead and chilled, ready for serving.

As we gathered on the porch of friends in Finland, we were served an appetizer: chilled champagne and the largest, sweetest peas in the pod, which we cracked open and ate like we would have eaten peanuts.

SUMMER SOUP | STRAWBERRY PUDDING

DILL BUTTERED NEW FINGERLING POTATOES

Real new potatoes are the first of the season: tiny, thumb-sized, with delicate jackets. Fingerling potatoes, which are now available, are as long and thick as your thumb, and may be yellow or red. Both are excellent prepared this way. Check the organic vegetable section for them.

- 3 lb. fingerling potatoes or tiny new potatoes
- Water
- 1 teaspoon salt
- 1/4 cup butter, melted
- 1 teaspoon chopped fresh dill
- 1/8 teaspoon salt
- Chopped fresh dill

1 In large saucepan, cover potatoes with enough water to barely cover potatoes; add 1 teaspoon salt. Simmer over medium heat 30 minutes or just until potatoes can be easily pierced with toothpick; avoid overcooking. Drain water from saucepan; return to heat. Shake pan to let potatoes dry well.

2 In small bowl, mix butter and 1 teaspoon dill.

3 Place hot potatoes in a warm bowl. Drizzle with dill butter; add salt to taste. Garnish with fresh dill.

8 servings.

SMOKED WHOLE SALMON

Fresh whole salmon takes on light smoke flavor in just one hour. If you have a smoker, use it, following the manufacturer's directions. Otherwise, you will need a covered barbecue to smoke this salmon.

SALMON
- 1 (7- to 8-lb.) whole salmon
- 2 to 3 tablespoons mixed pickling spices
- 2 tablespoons kosher (coarse) salt
- 1 teaspoon freshly ground pepper
- 1 large bunch fresh young dill sprigs
- 2 tablespoons vegetable oil

- 1 quart alder or hickory chips, soaked in water 1 hour or longer

GARNISH
- Fresh dill sprigs
- Lemon slices
- Butter lettuce leaves

1 Wipe salmon inside and out with paper towels. Sprinkle inside of fish with pickling spices, 1 teaspoon of the salt and pepper. Stuff with dill. Place in large pan; sprinkle outside of fish with remaining salt; cover. Refrigerate 1 hour or overnight.

2 Meanwhile, start charcoal grill. Place several handfuls of wood chips for smoking into bowl; cover with water. When coals are hot, rake them to the side, leaving center free of hot coals. Drain wood chips; sprinkle evenly over coals. Place rack in grill.

3 Rub both sides of fish with oil. Place fish on grill rack. Cover; leave vents half open so fish cooks and smokes slowly. Smoke-cook 45 to 60 minutes or until salmon flakes easily (or until a fin is easily pulled from fish).

4 Remove fish; place on serving platter. Score skin of fish lengthwise about 2 inches apart. Using a wooden pick, roll skin back toward tail.

5 Garnish with dill sprigs, lemon slices and lettuce leaves.

8 to 10 servings.

Smoked Whole Salmon

WILD MUSHROOM SAUCE

Finns consider wild mushrooms a major ingredient, especially during spring, summer and fall. This mushroom sauce is generally made with whatever mushrooms are being gathered at the time. You can use various wild mushrooms available in the supermarket produce section, and you can mix the varieties to get a full, rounded mushroom flavor. Serve this sauce with Smoked Whole Salmon (page 144).

- 2 tablespoons extra-virgin olive oil or vegetable oil
- 1 large sweet onion, finely chopped
- 4 garlic cloves, finely chopped
- 1 lb. wild mushrooms (mixture of shiitake, oyster, morels or other available mushrooms OR white button mushrooms), cleaned, coarsely chopped
- 1 cup dry white wine
- 1 teaspoon chopped or crumbled fresh sage
- 1 teaspoon dried thyme
- 1 teaspoon sugar
- 1 teaspoon salt
- 1/2 teaspoon freshly ground pepper
- 1/4 cup finely chopped fresh dill or 2 tablespoons dried
- 1 cup whipping cream

1 In large skillet or wok, heat oil over high heat. Add onion and garlic; sauté 2 to 3 minutes or until aromatic. Add mushrooms; reduce heat to medium-low. Cook 15 minutes. Add wine, sage, thyme, sugar, salt, pepper, dill and cream. Reduce heat to low; simmer 10 to 15 minutes until sauce is thickened. Adjust seasonings to taste. Serve warm with smoked salmon.

8 to 10 servings.

SUMMER SOUP

This soup is traditionally made with young, sweet, fresh vegetables — the first of the season. It's great served as a main course with fresh bread and cheese and is excellent reheated.

- 2 cups baby carrots, diced (1/2 inch)
- 1 1/2 cups small new potatoes, unpeeled, diced (1/2 inch)
- 1 cup snow peas, strings removed, cut diagonally (1/2 inch)
- 1 cup fresh baby green beans, cut into 1-inch pieces
- 1 bunch green onions, sliced (1/4 inch)

- 3 cups half-and-half or milk
- 1/3 cup all-purpose flour
- 1/4 cup butter
- 1 teaspoon sugar (if vegetables aren't very young)
- 1/8 teaspoon each salt
- 1/8 teaspoon freshly ground pepper
- 2 tablespoons finely chopped fresh dill or 2 teaspoons dried

1   In 3- to 4-quart saucepan, cover carrots and potatoes with boiling water. Bring to a boil; cook 10 minutes or until vegetables are tender. Add peas, green beans and onions. Simmer 5 minutes or until vegetables are tender.

2   Add all but 1/3 cup of the half-and-half. Mix flour into reserved 1/3 cup half-and-half to make a smooth paste; stir paste into soup. Simmer, stirring occasionally, about 10 minutes or until broth is slightly thickened.

3   Remove from heat; add butter, sugar, salt and pepper. Stir in dill.

8 main dish or 12 first course servings.

Summer Soup

STRAWBERRY PUDDING

While wild strawberries are the most authentic, local field-ripened berries also make a brilliant and fruity pudding.

3 lb. ripe, sweet, preferably field strawberries
3 cups water
1 cup plus 1 tablespoon sugar
1/4 cup potato starch
1 cup cold water
 Plain or whipped cream

1 Clean berries. Place prettiest ones — about 1/2 of them — into dessert bowl. Place remaining berries in saucepan; cover with 3 cups water. Bring to a boil; cover. Simmer 10 minutes or until berries are soft and liquid is red. Strain mixture; discard pulp. Return juice to saucepan. Add 1 cup of the sugar.

2 In small bowl, mix potato starch and cold water to make a smooth paste. Pour into juice, stirring well. Return pan to heat; simmer until pudding thickens and becomes transparent. Pour over whole strawberries in bowl. Sprinkle with remaining tablespoon sugar; cool.

3 Serve chilled with cream.

8 servings.

Strawberry Pudding

DO-AHEAD ASIAN COCKTAIL PARTY

Jean Yueh

CRISPY FRIED DUMPLINGS IN CHINESE SWEET AND SOUR DIPPING SAUCE | VIETNAMESE SALAD ROLLS WITH PEANUT DIPPING SAUCE

ecause many Asian dishes can be made ahead and refrigerated or frozen, they often adapt well as cocktail party finger food. An additional advantage is they can be easily made in large quantities, so they are perfect for entertaining.

You can set a festive Asian theme by serving all Asian hors d'oeuvres, or you can select one or two of these recipes to accent other appetizers. Either way, the ideas here will add a welcome change to your entertainment repertoire.

CHERRY TOMATOES FILLED WITH THAI FLAVORED MINCED BEEF | THAI FLAVORED MUSSELS ON HALF SHELLS | BAKED CURRY BEEF PUFFS

CRISPY FRIED DUMPLINGS IN CHINESE SWEET AND SOUR DIPPING SAUCE

To make light and crispy fried dumplings, it is important to use very thin wonton wrappers (80 to 100 sheets per 1-lb. package), which are available in Chinese markets. Thicker wrappers can be quite doughy after frying. Though they taste best freshly fried, these dumplings can be made ahead and refrigerated 3 to 4 days, or frozen several months. Defrost if frozen. Reheat them, turning once, in a preheated 325°F oven 15 to 20 minutes or until crispy. You'll get better results by heating them on a wire rack on a jelly roll pan, to allow hot air to circulate.

FILLING
- 1/2 lb. lean ground pork
- 1/2 lb. shelled, deveined uncooked medium shrimp, minced
- 4 teaspoons minced fresh ginger
- 2 teaspoons cornstarch
- 1 1/4 teaspoons salt or to taste
- 1/2 teaspoon sugar
- 1 tablespoon dry sherry
- 1 tablespoon Asian sesame oil or vegetable oil
- 8 water chestnuts, minced
- 2 scallions, minced (white part only)

DUMPLING
- 60 very thin wonton wrappers

SAUCE
- 2 tablespoons vegetable oil
- 1 tablespoon minced fresh ginger
- 1 tablespoon minced fresh garlic
- 1/2 teaspoon crushed red pepper or to taste (optional)
- 1/4 cup plus 2 teaspoons sugar or to taste
- 1/2 cup water
- 2 tablespoons plus 1 teaspoon soy sauce or to taste
- 2 tablespoons ketchup
- 2 tablespoons wine vinegar or to taste
- 2 teaspoons cornstarch stirred into 4 teaspoons water

- 3 cups vegetable oil for frying

1 In large bowl, combine pork, shrimp, 4 teaspoons ginger, cornstarch, salt, 1/2 teaspoon sugar, sherry, 1 tablespoon oil, chestnuts and scallions; stir until thoroughly mixed. Place 1 teaspoon filling in middle of each wrapper. Bring edges up over filling. Use a drop of water and pinch to seal filling, forming a small pouch.

2   To make sauce, in small saucepan, heat 2 tablespoons oil over medium heat until hot. Sauté 1 tablespoon ginger, garlic and crushed red pepper 30 seconds, taking care not to burn garlic. Add 1/4 cup plus 2 teaspoons sugar, water, soy sauce, ketchup and vinegar. Heat to a boil. Stir cornstarch mixture; add slowly to sauce, stirring constantly, until thickened.

3   In wok or large saucepan, heat oil for frying to 325°F. Fry several dumplings at a time about 2 minutes or until filling is cooked and wrappers are crispy and golden. Remove with slotted spoon or strainer; drain on paper towels. Keep dumplings warm in 200°F oven while frying remaining dumplings. Serve with sauce.

60 dumplings.

Crispy Fried Dumplings in Chinese Sweet and Sour Dipping Sauce

VIETNAMESE SALAD ROLLS WITH PEANUT DIPPING SAUCE

The aromatic herbs in these rolls lend a refreshing and delicate taste. For finger-size rolls, use 6 1/4-inch round rice paper. These salad rolls can be made a few hours in advance.

FILLING

1	large carrot, cut into matchstick-size strips
1	teaspoon sugar
24	(6 1/4-inch) round rice papers*
1	head Boston lettuce, washed, dried
2	cups cooked angel hair pasta
1/2	lb. cooked turkey breast, thinly sliced
50	fresh basil leaves or to taste
50	fresh mint leaves or to taste
1	bunch fresh coriander

DIPPING SAUCE

2	tablespoons vegetable oil
2	garlic cloves, minced
1	medium onion, minced
1/2	teaspoon crushed red pepper or to taste (optional)
1 1/2	cups reduced-sodium chicken broth or water
3	tablespoons soy sauce or to taste
3	tablespoons creamy peanut butter
4	teaspoons sugar or to taste
4	teaspoons tomato paste
1/2	teaspoon freshly ground pepper

1 In small bowl, mix carrot with 1 teaspoon sugar; let stand 15 minutes or until tender.

2 Fill large bowl with warm water. Work with 1 rice paper at a time, dipping it into warm water. Quickly remove; lay sheet flat on clean kitchen towel. If desired, wet several sheets and lay them on towel until they become pliable.

3 When sheet is soft and pliable, tear small piece of lettuce (do not use stem); lay it on bottom 1/3 of 1 rice paper. Place 1 level tablespoon noodles on top of lettuce. Top with a few carrot pieces, about 1 tablespoon turkey and 2 each of basil, mint and coriander leaves. Roll rice paper halfway into a cylinder. Fold both sides of paper over filling. Keep rolling to form a cylinder; seal edges. Repeat with remaining rolls. Place rolls sealed side down; cover with plastic wrap or damp towel. Store at room temperature. Serve rolls whole or cut in 1/2 just before serving. Serve with Peanut Dipping Sauce.

4 To make sauce, in small saucepan, heat oil over medium heat until hot. Add garlic and onion; sauté until onion is tender and transparent, taking care not to burn garlic. Add crushed red pepper; cook 30 seconds. Add broth, soy sauce, peanut butter, sugar, tomato paste and pepper; cook and stir until sauce is slightly thick and creamy. Add more peanut butter for thicker sauce; add more water for thinner sauce. Adjust seasonings to taste.

TIP *Rice paper can be purchased in Asian markets.

24 (about 3 1/4x1 1/2-inch) rolls.

CHERRY TOMATOES FILLED WITH THAI FLAVORED MINCED BEEF

Try to get large cherry tomatoes; you can stuff more filling into them. They will be attractive and more uniform on the serving platter if they are all the same size. The filling is a Thai-flavored beef salad. If you prefer, omit jalapeño pepper.

24 large cherry tomatoes

FILLING

1/2	lb. cooked beef or deli roast beef, minced (about 2 cups)
1/4	cup minced onion
2	teaspoons sugar
1/2	teaspoon freshly ground pepper or to taste
3	tablespoons minced fresh coriander or parsley
2	tablespoons minced red bell pepper
2	tablespoons minced jalapeño chile or to taste (optional)
1 1/2 to 2	tablespoons fish sauce* or to taste
1	tablespoon plus 2 teaspoons fresh lime juice or to taste

1 Trim about 1/8 inch from top of each tomato. Slice a tiny piece off bottom of each tomato to create a flat surface. (*Do not cut off too much or the filling will leak out.*) With tip of a small knife, gently loosen flesh around inside of each tomato. Scoop out seeds and pulp with small knife. Place tomatoes, open side down, on tray lined with several layers of paper towels to drain.

2 In large bowl, combine beef, onion, sugar, pepper, coriander, bell pepper, chile, fish sauce and lime juice; toss to mix. Adjust seasonings to taste. With small spoon, fill each tomato. Mound filling slightly above opening. Serve at room temperature. Filled tomatoes can be kept, covered and refrigerated, 1/2 a day.

TIP *Look for fish sauce, used throughout southeast Asia in much the same way as soy sauce, in the Asian section of supermarkets. If fish sauce is not available, replace with salt and soy sauce to taste.

24 cherry tomatoes.

THAI FLAVORED MUSSELS ON HALF SHELLS

This easy-to-make dish is flavored with lemon grass and fresh basil. Thai basil — available in Asian markets — is preferred. If unavailable, use sweet basil instead. When served on half shells, these mussels make attractive hors d'oeuvres.

  2   lb. mussels
  2   tablespoons vegetable oil
  2   shallots, minced
 1/2 teaspoon crushed red pepper or to taste
  2   cups water
  2   tablespoons fish sauce* or to taste
 1½   tablespoons fresh lime juice or to taste
  2   stalks lemongrass, cut into 1/2-
       inch sections
 30   Thai purple or sweet basil
       leaves, finely shredded
       Boston lettuce leaves

1 Wash and clean mussels with a brush, removing any hairy material. Discard opened mussels.

2 In large saucepan, heat oil over medium heat until hot. Add shallots and crushed red pepper; sauté about 1 minute. Add water, fish sauce, lime juice and lemongrass; bring to a boil. Simmer 1 minute. Add mussels and basil; cover. Cook about 2 minutes or until mussel shells open. Remove mussels from liquid with slotted spoon. Cool liquid to room temperature.

3 When mussels are cool, remove them from their shells. Place 1 mussel in each half shell; spoon cooled cooking liquid over each mussel. Arrange half shells on serving platter lined with lettuce leaves. Serve at room temperature.

> TIP *Look for fish sauce, used throughout southeast Asia in much the same way as soy sauce, in the Asian section of supermarkets.

Servings depend on size of mussel per pound.

Thai Flavored Mussels on Half Shells

BAKED CURRY BEEF PUFFS

These beef-filled pastries are usually sold at Chinese bakeries because traditional Chinese kitchens do not have ovens. The flaky pastry dough was originally made with lard and quite time consuming to make. In this recipe, we make a quick and easy variation using frozen ready-to-use puff pastry sheets (available in supermarkets). Puff pastry comes in a 17.3-oz. package in two pre-rolled sheets. This dough makes a crisper pastry, and it is also delicious.

FILLING

1	tablespoon vegetable oil
1/2	medium onion, finely chopped
1/2	lb. lean ground beef
1/2	cup mashed potato
2 1/2	teaspoons curry powder or to taste
1	teaspoon sugar
3/4	teaspoons salt or to taste
1/2	tablespoon soy sauce

PASTRY

1	(17.3-oz.) package frozen puff pastry sheets
1	egg yolk mixed with 1 teaspoon milk

1   In wok or large skillet, heat 1/2 tablespoon of the oil over medium heat until hot. Add onion; sauté until transparent but not wilted; remove from wok. Add remaining 1/2 tablespoon oil to wok; increase heat to high. Cook beef until it loses its reddish color. Return onion to wok; add potato, curry powder, sugar, salt and soy sauce. Cook and stir mixture thoroughly; cool before filling pastry.

2   Meanwhile, thaw pastry 40 minutes or until soft and easily unfolded. Cut each sheet along folds, making 3 (3x10-inch) rectangles; cut each rectangle into 8 (1 1/2x2 1/2-inch) pieces. (*You will have 24 pieces from each sheet for a total of 48.*)

3   Heat oven to 375°F. On lightly floured surface, use a rolling pin to roll each piece into 3 1/2-inch square. Place about 2 teaspoons filling in center of 1 square. Wet edges with water; fold square into a triangle. Press edges together to seal. Brush with egg yolk mixture. Repeat with remaining pastry and filling.

4   Place triangles on baking sheets; bake 20 minutes or until crust is baked and golden. Puffs can be made ahead and refrigerated or frozen. When ready to serve, reheat puffs in oven. Uncooked puffs can be frozen and baked in a preheated oven directly from freezer.

48 puffs.

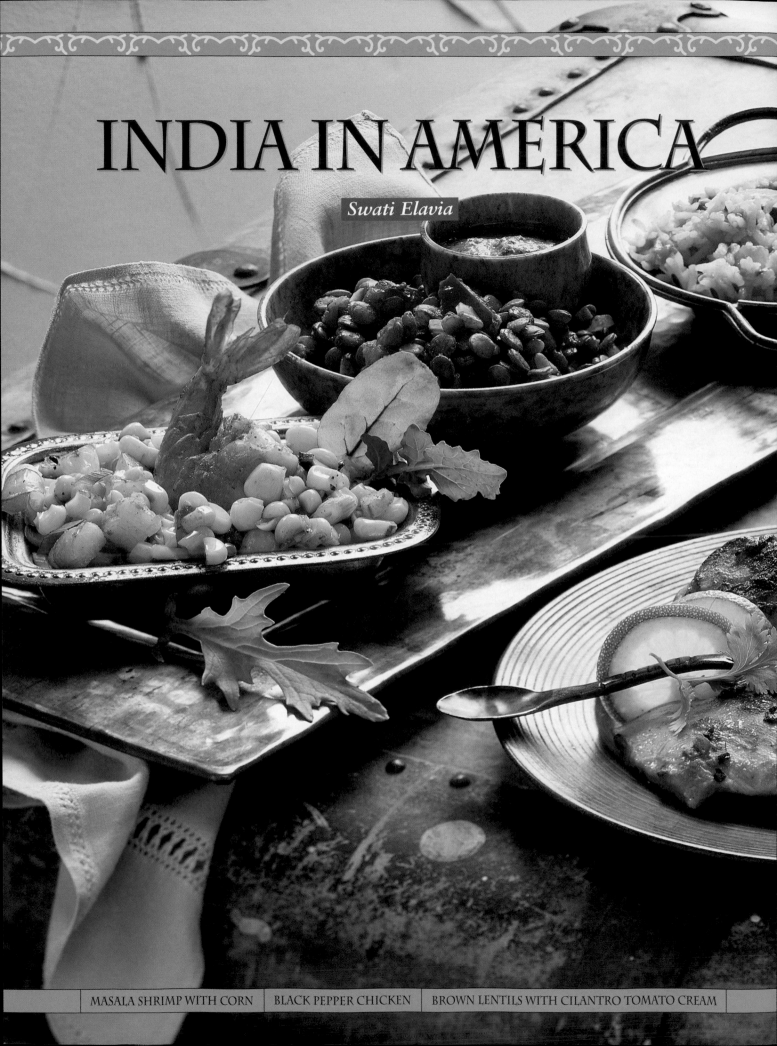

INDIA IN AMERICA

Swati Elavia

MASALA SHRIMP WITH CORN | BLACK PEPPER CHICKEN | BROWN LENTILS WITH CILANTRO TOMATO CREAM

lanning an Indian meal in America is far less restrictive than cooking in India. I can combine ingredients and techniques from other cuisines to enhance my own culinary repertoire. When I started planning this menu, I wanted to have lots of different foods with bold flavors. I wanted delicate presentation of Indian food that you would want to offer to friends and family. I also wanted to design a menu that had no mention of curry but still presented all the flavors that Indian cooking has to offer.

Although my recipes have their origin in traditional Indian cooking, their presentation is cross-cultural. For example the Masala Shrimp with Corn recipe is prepared in a traditional Indian way but enjoys some texture and color with lettuce and tortilla triangles. Black Pepper Chicken is made with minimal ingredients and spices but offers a very tantalizing combination of hot, sour and sweet tastes. Lentils are enhanced with the cilantro-tomato cream; otherwise they are quite boring looking. My favorite way of cooking cauliflower is with lots of ginger, fennel and colorful bell peppers; this produces pungent flavors and avoids the monochromatic look that most Indian vegetables have. Tomato Rice Pilaf satisfies my personal need to have a lot of different color on the table. Tomatoes also add a sour note to the nutty taste of basmati rice, and the whole dish is very delectable.

I hope you enjoy all these recipes, and make Indian cuisine a part of your own culinary repertoire.

CAULIFLOWER WITH GREEN AND RED PEPPERS | TOMATO RICE PILAF

MASALA SHRIMP WITH CORN

When corn is available in abundance in India, a spicy mouth-watering snack of corn kernels is made as in this recipe. I always like to stretch the traditional recipes, and that's where the masala shrimp (well-seasoned shrimp) makes it a new dish altogether. It can be served as an appetizer on fried corn tortillas or on a salad of mesclun greens.

SHRIMP

- 1 teaspoon fresh lime juice
- 1 teaspoon minced fresh ginger
- 1/2 teaspoon minced fresh garlic
- 1/2 teaspoon ground cumin
- 1/4 teaspoon salt
- 1/8 teaspoon freshly ground pepper
- 1/8 teaspoon crushed red pepper
  Dash ground cloves
- 1 tablespoon vegetable oil
- 1/2 lb. shelled, deveined uncooked medium shrimp

CORN

- 1 tablespoon vegetable oil
- 1 teaspoon minced serrano chile
- 1 1/2 cups fresh corn kernels (corn of 2 cobs)
- 2 tablespoons water
- 1 teaspoon fresh lime juice
- 1/4 teaspoon salt
- 1 tablespoon chopped green onion (green part only)

SALAD DRESSING

- 1/4 cup vegetable oil
- 3 tablespoons rice vinegar
- 1 tablespoon fresh orange juice
- 1 teaspoon minced fresh ginger
- 1/4 teaspoon sugar
- 1/4 teaspoon salt
- 1/4 teaspoon toasted ground cumin*
- 1/8 teaspoon cayenne pepper

TORTILLA CHIPS

Vegetable oil for frying
Tortillas**

GARNISH

Chopped salad greens

1 In large bowl, combine 1 teaspoon lime juice, 1 teaspoon ginger, garlic, 1/2 teaspoon cumin, 1/4 teaspoon salt, freshly ground pepper, crushed red pepper, cloves and 1 tablespoon oil; mix well. Place shrimp in marinade; refrigerate, covered, 45 minutes.

2 Remove shrimp from marinade; discard marinade. Heat large skillet over medium-high heat until hot. Add shrimp; sauté 5 minutes or until shrimp turn pink. Remove shrimp from skillet; set aside.

3 In same skillet, heat 1 tablespoon oil over medium-high heat until hot. Add chile; sauté 30 seconds. Stir in corn; sauté an additional 4 to 5 minutes. Add water, 1 teaspoon lime juice and 1/4 teaspoon salt; cook until water is absorbed and corn is cooked but not mushy. Stir in green onion. Remove from skillet; set aside.

4 For dressing, in large bowl, whisk together 1/4 cup oil, vinegar, orange juice, 1 teaspoon ginger, sugar, 1/4 teaspoon salt, toasted cumin and cayenne pepper.

5 In same skillet, heat oil for frying over medium-high heat until hot. Cut tortilla into 8 wedges; fry until crisp. Set aside.

Masala Shrimp with Corn

6 Chop shrimp into small pieces; mix well with corn and 2 tablespoons dressing. Place 1 spoonful of shrimp-corn mixture on each tortilla chip. Garnish with greens and remaining dressing. OR, divide greens among salad plates. Arrange $1/2$ cup corn mixture in center of each; surround with about 4 whole shrimp. Drizzle dressing over salads; serve each with 1 or 2 tortilla chips standing on the side.

TIPS *To toast cumin: In skillet, stir cumin seeds over medium heat until brown; grind in coffee grinder.

**You can also use wonton squares cut into 2 triangles.

6 servings.

BLACK PEPPER CHICKEN

This dish has its origin in southern India. People there have a higher threshold for spicy food than anywhere else in India. The region also produces the most black pepper. This dish offers the perfect combination of aroma and freshly ground black pepper. A spicy sour taste is delicately balanced with the light sweetness of coconut milk. Serve with tomato rice pilaf or simply a bowl of boiled white rice and you will be fully satisfied.

1	teaspoon minced fresh ginger		1/2	teaspoon salt
1	teaspoon minced fresh garlic		1 1/2	lb. boneless skinless chicken thighs, halved
3	tablespoons malt or white vinegar		1	large yellow onion
1	tablespoon fresh lime juice		3	tablespoons vegetable oil
1	teaspoon freshly ground pepper		1/4	cup coconut milk
1/2	teaspoon ground turmeric		1/4	cup chopped fresh cilantro

1   In large bowl, combine ginger, garlic, vinegar, lime juice, pepper, turmeric and salt; mix well. Place chicken in marinade; cover. Refrigerate 30 minutes.

2   Cut 1/2 of the onion into thin slices. In food processor, puree remaining 1/2 onion.

3   In large skillet, heat oil over medium heat until hot. Add sliced onion; sauté 5 minutes. Add pureed onion; sauté an additional 7 to 8 minutes or until onions are golden brown.

4   Remove chicken from marinade; discard marinade. Add chicken to skillet; simmer, covered, 20 minutes or until chicken is no longer pink in center.

5   Add coconut milk; cook, uncovered, an additional 5 to 7 minutes. Add cilantro; mix well. Serve hot.

6 servings.

Black Pepper Chicken

BROWN LENTILS WITH CILANTRO TOMATO CREAM

Although Indian cooking offers an exciting array of lentil dishes, they have not received much attention in the gourmet world. To satisfy the discriminating palate of my own family and friends, I have always tried to make lentils something more than the simple dals (peas, lentils or beans) that I grew up on. A little garnish of cilantro-tomato cream changes the way this lentil dish is perceived. I also like the different flavor that the cream adds to the one-dimensional flavor of lentils. You can serve this as a soup too.

LENTILS

- 1 cup brown lentils
- 6 cups water
- 3/4 teaspoon salt
- 2 tablespoons vegetable oil
- 1/2 cup chopped yellow onion
- 1 teaspoon minced fresh garlic
- 1 cup chopped tomatoes
- 1/4 teaspoon ground turmeric
- 1/2 teaspoon cayenne pepper
- 1/2 teaspoon garam masala*

CREAM

- 1/4 cup plain yogurt
- 1 tablespoon fresh lime juice
- 1 cup chopped fresh cilantro
- 1/2 cup chopped tomato
- 1 teaspoon minced fresh ginger
- 1/2 teaspoon sugar
- 1/2 teaspoon cumin seeds
- 1/4 teaspoon salt

1 In medium bowl, soak lentils in 3 cups of the water 15 minutes; drain.

2 In large saucepan, combine lentils with remaining 3 cups water. Add salt; bring to a boil over medium-high heat. Reduce heat to low; simmer 25 minutes, half covered to prevent lentils from boiling over.

3 In large skillet, heat oil over medium-high heat. Add onion; sauté 5 to 7 minutes or until onion is brown. Add garlic; sauté an additional 2 minutes. Add tomatoes; cook until tender. Add turmeric and cayenne pepper; cook 30 seconds. Stir in cooked lentils and garam masala; simmer an additional 5 minutes or until warm and well mixed.

4 In large bowl, combine yogurt, lime juice, cilantro, tomato, ginger, sugar, cumin seeds and salt; mix well. Add water to thin this sauce, if needed.

5 Swirl cream mixture over cooked lentils. Garnish with additional chopped tomatoes or fresh cilantro sprigs.

TIP *Garam masala is a blend of up to 12 spices, including cinnamon, cloves, cumin and pepper. It is available in most grocery stores under the Spice Hunter brand or other commercial brands.

6 servings.

CAULIFLOWER WITH GREEN AND RED PEPPERS

Cauliflower is one of my favorite vegetables, and I cook it often. But the traditional way of cooking cauliflower lends an unappetizing pale yellow color to the dish. Adding red and green bell pepper strips makes the color of this dish more appetizing. Tempering cauliflower with fennel seeds creates an interesting aroma which you don't get with any other spice. Leftovers make a substantial hot or cold sandwich filling.

1/2 head cauliflower, cut into 1-inch florets
2 tablespoons vegetable oil
1 teaspoon fennel seeds
2 serrano peppers, halved lengthwise
1 tablespoon matchstick-size strips fresh ginger ($1/8$x$1/8$x$2^1/2$-inch)
1/2 teaspoon salt
1/8 teaspoon ground turmeric
1/8 teaspoon cayenne pepper
2 tablespoons water
1/3 cup matchstick-size strips red bell pepper ($1/8$x$1/8$x$2^1/2$-inch)
1/3 cup matchstick-size strips green bell pepper ($1/8$x$1/8$x$2^1/2$-inch)
1 tablespoon chopped fresh cilantro
1/2 teaspoon garam masala (see page 163)

1 Rinse cauliflower florets; pat dry.

2 Heat large skillet over medium heat until hot. Add fennel seeds; sauté 30 seconds. Add serranos, ginger and cauliflower; sauté 5 minutes. Stir in salt, turmeric and cayenne pepper, mixing well. Add water; cover. Simmer 10 minutes, stirring occasionally.

3 Add bell peppers, cilantro and garam masala; cook an additional 2 minutes before serving.

6 servings.

Cauliflower with Green and Red Peppers

Tomato Rice Pilaf

TOMATO RICE PILAF

The beautiful color of this wonderful pilaf comes from tomatoes and red chili powder. Serve with a traditional Indian meal or simply enjoy with plain yogurt. I also eat it cold as rice salad with some greens.

1	cup basmati rice
4 1/2	cups water
2	tablespoons vegetable oil
1	teaspoon cumin seeds
1/2	cup sliced yellow onion
1	tomato, chopped fine
1	serrano chile
1/2	teaspoon salt
1/2	teaspoon paprika
10	cherry tomatoes, halved
1	tablespoon fresh lemon juice

1 In medium bowl, soak rice in 3 cups of the water 20 minutes; drain.

2 In large saucepan, heat oil over medium-high heat until hot. Sauté cumin 30 seconds or until brown. Add onion; sauté 5 to 7 minutes or until brown. Reduce heat to medium; sauté tomato and chile 3 to 4 minutes. Stir in rice, salt, paprika, cherry tomatoes and lemon juice; cook 2 minutes. Reduce heat to low. Add remaining 1 1/2 cups water; simmer 15 to 20 minutes or until water is absorbed and rice is cooked.

6 servings.

TOURING ITALY

Michele Anna Jordan

SALAD OF SHAVED CELERY, PARMIGIANO AND OLIVE OIL WITH FETTUNTA | FETTUCCINE WITH SMOKED SALMON, CREAM AND VODKA

The renowned Waverly Root, *who wrote so lovingly of the cuisines of both France and Italy, believed that any region's cuisine could be understood by looking at the primary fat used. In northern France, for example, where weather is inhospitable to both olive and walnut trees, butter shapes the flavors and techniques of the kitchen. In areas where walnut trees thrive, walnut oil lends a unique character to the cooking. Travel a bit farther south, and olive trees begin to cover the landscape; where the trees thrive, their fruit and its oil shape the area's cuisine.*

Today we are not limited to the type of fat our immediate area can offer us, yet the traditional regional foods we continue to enjoy evolved during a time when it was virtually impossible to send perishable ingredients far from their home.

This menu celebrates both the wonderful olive oil that has long been essential to Italian cuisine, as well as the butter and cream that are so readily available today. You'll notice that pasta is not the centerpiece of this menu, as it tends to be in America. Rather, it is presented as a first course, as it so often is in Italy.

LAMB SCALOPPINE WITH LEMON AND FRIED CAPERS   ROASTED ASPARAGUS WITH PARMIGIANO AND GARLIC BREAD CRUMBS   RICOTTA CAKE

SALAD OF SHAVED CELERY, PARMIGIANO AND OLIVE OIL WITH FETTUNTA

Celery prepared in this way is both delicious and refreshing, a wonderfully light start to the rich meal that follows.

7 to 8	ribs celery, trimmed, sliced diagonally (1/8 to 1/16 inch)
1/8	teaspoon kosher (coarse) salt, plus more to taste
1/8	teaspoon freshly ground pepper, plus more to taste
2	tablespoons extra-virgin olive oil, plus more for fettunta
1	(1-lb.) loaf country-style Italian bread, sliced (1/2 inch thick)
6	large garlic cloves, halved lengthwise
1	(3- to 4-oz.) chunk Parmigiano-Reggiano cheese

1 In medium bowl, season celery lightly with salt and pepper; drizzle with 2 tablespoons olive oil. Toss gently; divide among individual serving plates.

2 Heat stove-top grill or broiler; toast bread until golden brown on both sides. Rub cut side of garlic clove firmly into 1 side of toasted bread, covering entire surface. Repeat, using new piece of garlic for each slice of toast, until all toast has been rubbed with garlic.

3 Using a vegetable peeler, top celery with cheese curls. Add 1 or 2 slices toast to each serving. Drizzle with olive oil; season with salt and pepper. Serve immediately.

6 servings.

FETTUCCINE WITH SMOKED SALMON, CREAM AND VODKA

Pasta with a sauce of cream, tomato and vodka is a classic Italian dish. In this version, smoked salmon adds a luscious and festive element.

12	oz. smoked salmon (lox), thinly sliced
	Grated peel of 1 lemon
1/3	cup vodka
1/8	teaspoon freshly ground pepper, plus more to taste
1	tablespoon kosher (coarse) salt, plus more to taste
1	lb. fettuccine
1 1/2	cups heavy cream
3	tablespoons tomato paste
2	tablespoons minced fresh Italian parsley
	Small fresh Italian parsley sprigs

1   Cut salmon into 1/2-inch wide strips; place in small, wide bowl. Sprinkle with lemon peel. Drizzle with 1/2 of the vodka; season with pepper. Toss gently; set aside.

2   Fill large pot 2/3 full of water; add 1 tablespoon salt. Bring to a boil over high heat. Cook fettuccine in boiling water until just tender. Drain thoroughly but do not rinse. Place pasta in wide, shallow bowl.

3   Meanwhile, in small saucepan, heat cream over medium-low heat. Stir in tomato paste. Simmer 10 minutes or until cream is just slightly reduced. Stir in remaining vodka and minced parsley; season with salt and pepper. Remove from heat.

4   Set aside several strips of salmon for garnish; sprinkle remainder on top of hot pasta. Pour hot cream sauce over pasta; toss gently to thoroughly coat. Divide pasta among 6 individual plates. Season with pepper; garnish with salmon strips and parsley sprigs. Serve immediately.

6 servings.

Fettuccine with Smoked Salmon, Cream and Vodka

LAMB SCALOPPINE WITH LEMON AND FRIED CAPERS

Veal is the traditional meat in a lemony scaloppine, but lamb is wonderful prepared in the same way.

6	(8- to 10-oz.) lamb chops, trimmed of excess fat
2/3	cup all-purpose flour
1/8	teaspoon kosher (coarse) salt, plus more to taste
1/8	teaspoon freshly ground pepper, plus more to taste
3	tablespoons clarified butter
1	cup chicken stock or broth
1/4	cup fresh lemon juice
2	tablespoons unsalted butter, cut into 4 pieces, chilled
	Olive oil
3	tablespoons capers, drained

1 Place lamb on work surface; remove bones using a paring knife. Cut each lamb chop in half lengthwise using sharp chef's knife. (Depending on type of chop, each one may separate into pieces.) Use palm of one hand to gently press on meat while slicing. Set 1 piece of lamb between two sheets of wax paper; pound gently with meat tenderizer or French rolling pin until very thin. Repeat until all lamb has been pounded.

2 In medium bowl, combine flour, salt and pepper. Dredge each piece of lamb in mixture, shaking off excess flour.

3 In medium skillet, heat 1½ tablespoons of the clarified butter over medium-high heat until melted. Cook several slices of lamb, in single layer, 2 to 3 minutes or until meat begins to shrink slightly. Turn; cook 2 minutes more or until lightly browned. Transfer to warm serving plate. Cook remaining lamb, adding remaining clarified butter as needed.

4 When all of the lamb has been cooked, increase heat to high. Add stock; stir to loosen any bits of meat that stick to pan. Simmer until stock reduces to about ½ cup; add lemon juice. When mixture simmers, reduce heat to low.

Lamb Scaloppine with Lemon and Fried Capers

Add chilled butter, 1 piece at a time, swirling after each addition until just melted. Do not let sauce boil. When final piece of butter is melted, season with salt and pepper; pour sauce over lamb. Return pan to heat; add olive oil. Heat until oil is hot but not smoking. Fry capers 30 to 45 seconds or until they open. Transfer capers to absorbent paper using slotted spoon; sprinkle over lamb. Serve immediately.

6 servings.

ROASTED ASPARAGUS WITH PARMIGIANO AND GARLIC BREAD CRUMBS

When asparagus is roasted rather than steamed or boiled, its flavors are concentrated and intensified. An added bonus is that, when cooked this way, the stalks don't need to be peeled.

1 1/2	lb. asparagus, tough stems snapped off
3	tablespoons olive oil
1/8	teaspoon kosher (coarse) salt
1/8	teaspoon freshly ground pepper
1	cup coarse fresh bread crumbs*
3	garlic cloves, pressed
2	oz. (1/2 cup) freshly grated Parmigiano-Reggiano cheese

1 Heat oven to 475°F. Place asparagus on baking sheet; drizzle with 2 tablespoons of the oil. Toss lightly with your fingers until asparagus is coated. Season with salt pepper. Bake until asparagus is just tender, 7 to 8 minutes for thin spears or 12 minutes for thicker ones.

2 Meanwhile, put bread crumbs in small glass jar or plastic container; add garlic and remaining tablespoon oil. Cover tightly; shake to evenly distribute garlic and oil. In small skillet, sauté bread crumbs over medium heat, stirring constantly, until golden brown and just crisp. Remove from heat.

3 Arrange asparagus on serving platter; top with bread crumbs and cheese. Serve immediately.

> TIP *To make fresh bread crumbs, tear 2 to 3 thick slices of two-day-old bread into pieces. In food processor, pulse bread pieces into coarse crumbs. Repeat until all the bread crumbs have been made.

4 to 6 servings.

Roasted Asparagus with Parmigiano and Garlic Bread Crumbs

Ricotta Cake

RICOTTA CAKE

Fresh ricotta is light and delicious; be sure to use it for this delicate cheesecake.

CRUST

- 1/2 cup unsalted butter, softened
- 1/4 cup sugar
- 1/2 teaspoon vanilla
- 1 1/4 cups all-purpose flour
- 1/4 teaspoon kosher (coarse) salt
- 3/4 cup toasted walnuts

FILLING

- 1 lb. fresh ricotta cheese
- 3/4 cup sugar
- 1 egg
- 2 egg yolks
- 1/2 teaspoon vanilla
- 1 cup heavy cream

1 To make crust, in food processor, pulse butter and 1/4 cup sugar until well blended. Add 1/2 teaspoon vanilla, flour and salt; pulse until flour and butter are well combined. Add walnuts; pulse several times. Transfer dough to sheet of plastic wrap; wrap tightly. Refrigerate 1 hour.

2 Heat oven to 400°F. Press chilled dough into 9- or 10-inch springform pan; bake 15 to 20 minutes or until crust is lightly browned. Cool completely.

3 Reduce oven to 350°F. In large bowl, mix ricotta and 3/4 cup sugar with wooden spoon. Stir in egg, egg yolks and 1/2 teaspoon vanilla. Stir in cream until mixture is smooth. Pour into cooled crust.

4 Bake about 45 to 65 minutes or until center is just set. Remove from oven; cool to room temperature. Remove springform ring. Cover; cool 2 to 3 hours before serving. Store in refrigerator.

6 to 8 servings.

PATIO PARTY FROM THE YUCATAN

Lisa Golden Schroeder

HIBISCUS COCKTAILS | SEA BASS WITH ACHIOTE SAUCE | ARROZ CON CILANTRO

The Yucatan peninsula of southern Mexico juts out into the Gulf of Mexico, and features dishes that celebrate the abundance of fresh seafood and produce. A unique seasoning from the region is achiote paste, made from the seeds of the annato tree. Fish baked in banana leaves with achiote paste (pibil) is a specialty. In this menu, sea bass is marinated in a spicy-tart mixture of ground achiote, allspice, oregano, lime and orange juices, then broiled or grilled.

Introduce guests to this casual dinner party with a crimson cocktail made from dried hibiscus flowers, and offer a selection of Mexican beer on the patio or deck. While the fish is grilling, bake the rice, aromatic with ground coriander, toasted cumin and fresh cilantro. Just before serving, toss together a unique combination of roasted green chile strips (which can be done beforehand) and steamed spinach, given a Spanish touch with garlic, toasted pine nuts and raisins. Then sit back and enjoy the sunset with a smooth coffee-orange caramel custard (flan).

RAJAS Y ESPINACAS (CHILES AND SPINACH)   ORANGE CAFE FLAN

HIBISCUS COCKTAILS

Tropical hibiscus flower petals (or actually the deep-red calyxes that cover the flower blossoms before they open) are dried in Mexico, and are called jamaica. *When steeped in hot water like a tea, the petals release an alluring crimson color and a tart, perfumy flavor. Sweetened and diluted with sparkling wine or mineral water, hibiscus beverages are easy to make for entertaining and give flexibility for nonalcoholic and alcoholic offerings. Jamaica punch is a New Year's tradition in Mexico.*

6   cups water
2   cups dried hibiscus flowers
3/4 cup honey
2   cinnamon sticks
2   tablespoons lemon juice
    Chilled sparkling mineral water or sparkling rosé wine
    Thin slices lemon or lime, if desired

1   In 4-quart saucepan, combine water, hibiscus flowers, honey and cinnamon sticks. Bring to a boil, stirring occasionally. Reduce heat to low; simmer, uncovered, 5 minutes. Remove from heat; let stand 20 minutes.

2   Strain liquid into large pitcher, pressing on solids to extract as much liquid as possible. Stir in lemon juice. Refrigerate at least 2 hours or until cold. For each serving, pour about 1/2 cup mixture into each glass over ice. Stir in about 1/2 cup mineral water. Garnish with lemon or lime slices.

8 to 10 servings.

Hibiscus Cocktails

Sea Bass with Achiote Sauce

SEA BASS WITH ACHIOTE SAUCE

The seasoning paste made from brick red achiote seeds is taken to an art form in the Yucatan. Achiote paste can be bought ready-made in Mexican markets, but it's easy to make at home — and much more flavorful. Grind the seeds and whole allspice in a spice grinder or clean coffee grinder until very finely powdered. This ensures that the paste will be smooth and less grainy on the tongue. A deep rust color is imparted to any food seasoned with achiote, along with an earthy aroma. Red snapper or halibut can be substituted for the sea bass.

MARINADE

3/4	cup fresh orange juice
1/2	cup fresh lime juice
2	tablespoons achiote (annato) seeds, finely ground
2	teaspoons whole allspice, finely ground
1 1/2	teaspoons dried Mexican oregano
1/2	teaspoon salt
1/2	teaspoon coarsely ground pepper
6	garlic cloves, halved
1	red or green jalapeño chile, seeded, coarsely chopped

FISH

6	(6-oz.) sea bass fillets
	Lime wedges

1 In blender, combine orange juice, lime juice, achiote seeds, allspice, oregano, salt, pepper, garlic and chiles; blend until smooth. Place fish in large resealable plastic bag. Add marinade to bag; seal bag. Turn bag to coat fish. (*Or place fish in large baking dish; pour marinade over. Turn occasionally.*) Refrigerate at least 30 minutes or up to 3 hours.

2 Heat grill or broiler. Remove fish from marinade; discard marinade. Place fish on hot grill. Cook, turning once, 10 minutes or until fish flakes easily with a fork. Serve fish with lime wedges.

6 servings.

ARROZ CON CILANTRO

Rice (arroz) is a staple in Mexican cuisine, along with fresh tortillas. Coriander, the seeds of the cilantro plant, lends a different dimension to this oven-baked rice. Be sure to lightly toast the cumin seeds in a dry skillet, just until aromatic, before stirring them in for a burst of flavor. Cooked garbanzo or black beans gently folded into the rice after baking would be a nice addition to this dish.

1	tablespoon olive oil
1¹/2	cups long-grain rice
1	large onion, chopped
3	cups chicken broth or water
1	teaspoon salt
¹/2	teaspoon ground coriander
¹/2	cup chopped fresh cilantro
1	tablespoon grated lemon peel
1	teaspoon toasted cumin seeds*

1 Heat oven to 350°F. In ovenproof casserole or Dutch oven, heat oil over medium-high heat until hot. Add rice and onion; sauté 3 minutes. Stir in broth, salt and coriander; bring to a boil. Remove from heat; cover tightly.

2 Bake rice mixture 35 to 40 minutes or until rice is tender. Remove from oven; let stand, covered, 5 minutes.

3 Sprinkle cilantro, lemon peel and cumin seeds over rice. Gently fluff rice mixture with fork, stirring in seasonings.

TIP *To toast cumin seeds, in skillet, stir seeds over medium-heat until brown and aromatic, about 3 minutes.

6 servings.

RAJAS Y ESPINACAS

CHILES AND SPINACH

Roasted green chile strips (rajas) are an essential flavor of the Mexican kitchen. The distinctive smoky flavor of roasted chiles combines well with quickly sautéed spinach and garlic. Cotijo is an aged hard cheese, reminiscent of Parmesan, and is a delicious counterpoint to the sweet raisins and pine nuts. Make this recipe easily by roasting the chiles ahead of time and using bags of washed organic baby spinach.

4	large poblano or Anaheim chiles
2	tablespoons olive oil
1/3	cup pine nuts
4	garlic cloves, minced
1/2	cup golden raisins
1	lb. baby spinach leaves (about 10 cups), cleaned well
1	teaspoon water
	Salt and freshly ground pepper to taste
	Freshly grated cotijo or Parmesan cheese

1 To roast chiles, hold over open gas flame, turning frequently until skin is completely blistered and charred. OR, cut chiles in half lengthwise. Place cut-side down on baking sheet; broil until skin is blistered and charred. Place chiles in heavy resealable plastic food bag; seal bag. Let stand until cool enough to handle. Scrape blackened skin off chiles with paring knife. Remove stems and seeds; slice into 1/2-inch wide strips. Set aside.

2 In large deep skillet or Dutch oven, heat oil over medium heat until hot. Add pine nuts and garlic; sauté 2 minutes or until pine nuts are golden brown.

3 Add raisins to pan; sauté 30 seconds. Add spinach leaves and water. Cover pan; cook, tossing occasionally, until spinach is wilted. Stir in chile strips. Season with salt and pepper. Serve hot with cheese.

6 servings.

ORANGE CAFE FLAN

Coffee, orange and caramel — a sophisticated blend for a simple custard! Vary these flavors by using fresh tangerine juice for the milk, and grated tangerine peel instead of orange peel. To create the silky texture of a flan, bake in a water bath that keeps the heat constant and gentle.

1	cup sugar
3	tablespoons water
6	large eggs
3/4	cup half-and-half
1/4	cup milk
3	tablespoons Kahlúa or other coffee liqueur
1	tablespoon grated orange peel
1/2	teaspoon Mexican vanilla
	Thin slices orange, if desired

1 Heat oven to 350°F. Pour 1/2 inch hot water into roasting pan. Place in oven.

2 In small, heavy saucepan, mix 3/4 cup of the sugar and water. Stir until sugar dissolves. Place over high heat; cook syrup, swirling pan occasionally, until clear and amber colored. Immediately pour caramel syrup into 9-inch glass pie plate. Tilt and swirl dish to evenly coat bottom and halfway up sides. Set aside to cool and harden.

3 In medium bowl, lightly beat eggs. Whisk in remaining 1/4 cup sugar, half-and-half, milk, coffee liqueur, orange peel and vanilla; mix until well blended. Pour into pie plate.

4 Carefully place dish in hot water in oven. Bake about 25 minutes or until knife inserted in center comes out clean. Remove dish from hot water. Cover; refrigerate at least 6 hours or overnight.

5 To unmold, loosen edge of flan with tip of knife. Cover dish with 10-inch rimmed plate. Invert quickly. Caramel syrup will run over top of flan (*scrape any clinging caramel onto flan*). Cut into wedges; serve with sauce. Garnish with orange slices. Store in refrigerator.

6 servings.

Orange Café Flan

INDEX